I0814286

COLLEGE SPORTS ENCYCLOPEDIAS

# THE WOMEN'S COLLEGE BASKETBALL ENCYCLOPEDIA

BY LUKE HANLON

Encyclopedias

An Imprint of Abdo Reference

abdobooks.com

# TABLE OF CONTENTS

# THE HISTORY OF WOMEN'S COLLEGE BASKETBALL

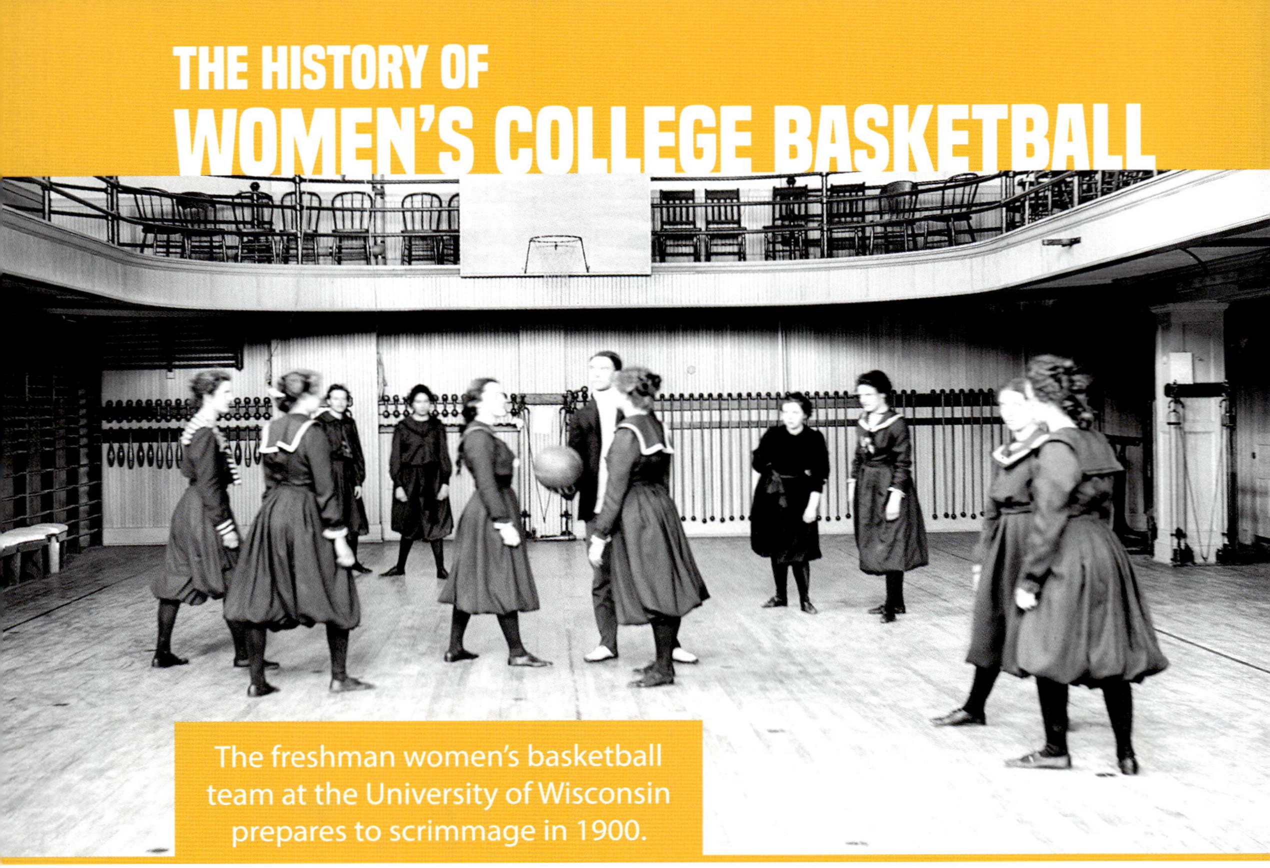

The freshman women's basketball team at the University of Wisconsin prepares to scrimmage in 1900.

In 1891, James Naismith invented the game of basketball to keep the boys in his physical education class busy during the long winters in Springfield, Massachusetts. The new game appealed to Senda Berenson, the head of physical education at the all-girls Smith College in nearby Northampton, Massachusetts. So, in 1892, she formed a women's basketball team at Smith.

Berenson's version of basketball looked much different than the game played today. Originally the court was divided into three sections, and players had to stay within their designated section. Each player could complete only three dribbles at a time. This encouraged less individual movement and more passing. The original uniforms looked much different too. Women wore floor-length dresses while playing basketball.

## LET THE GAMES BEGIN

On March 22, 1893, Smith College hosted the first official women's basketball game. Men weren't allowed in the school's gym to watch a group of sophomores take on a team of freshmen. An excited crowd of fellow students saw the sophomores win.

In the early years of women's basketball, players often wore blouses on the court.

Female students at UCLA shoot at a basketball hoop during the early 1900s.

Soon, Berenson's rules spread to other schools across the country. By the end of 1893, four other colleges formed women's teams. By 1896, women's basketball had spread all the way to the West Coast. That year, Stanford played against California in the first intercollegiate women's basketball game. Stanford won 2–1.

While basketball quickly became popular among women, much of society shunned women's sports at the time. Critics deemed basketball unladylike and too physical for women. Even some female physical educators didn't approve of the sport being played competitively. Instead, they wanted basketball to be viewed as an activity to promote an active lifestyle. Such opinions led schools such as Stanford and California to ban women's intercollegiate team sports in 1899.

## EARLY ORGANIZERS

The backlash against women's basketball continued into the early 1900s. Despite this, more schools started their own teams. Varsity competitions between schools were rare. Instead, teams mostly participated in intramural games against fellow students from their school.

By 1926, the Amateur Athletic Union (AAU) began hosting a tournament, which used men's basketball rules, to crown a women's basketball national champion. However, most of the teams that took part in the annual tournament were club teams sponsored by corporations. By the end of the 1920s, only 12 percent of colleges had varsity women's college basketball teams.

Throughout the next few decades, the rules of women's basketball frequently changed. By 1938, the three zones of the court were gone. Instead of nine players per team, games featured six players per team, with three from each team limited to one half of the court. Competitive games were played under these rules until 1971, when organizers officially

The women's basketball team at New York University practices in 1932.

Old Dominion, *shown in 1970*, was the first school in Virginia to offer scholarships in women's sports. The Lady Monarchs became an early power in women's basketball.

adopted the modern full-court, five-on-five format that the men used.

Another major shift in women's sports took place the next year. In 1972, the US government passed Title IX, which required federally funded education programs to offer equal opportunities to men and women. Though Title IX was geared toward education, it ultimately had a major effect on sports as well. With schools required to have girls' and women's teams, participation rates took off.

## FOR WOMEN, BY WOMEN

The National Collegiate Athletic Association (NCAA) had long governed men's college sports. Shortly before Title IX passed, a group of female administrators founded the Association for Intercollegiate Athletics for Women (AIAW). Their goal was to have a governing body that prioritized women. AIAW rules barred coaches from recruiting off their own campuses.

Coach Cathy Rush designs a play for her Immaculata Mighty Macs ahead of a 1973 game.

Recruits were also required to pay for their own school visits. These rules were intended to avoid the scandals that sometimes plagued the NCAA.

The first AIAW basketball season ended with an unlikely champion. Immaculata, a small women-only school near Philadelphia, won the 1972 AIAW Tournament despite not having a home court on its campus. Future Basketball Hall of Famer Cathy Rush coached the Mighty Macs, and she turned them into women's college basketball's first dynasty. Her Immaculata teams went on to win the first three AIAW championships, a run that included an undefeated season in 1972–73. The Basketball Hall of Fame later enshrined the Mighty Macs teams of this era.

The Mighty Macs returned to the AIAW championship game in 1975 and 1976 as well. However, a new dynasty upended Immaculata. Delta State, a small school in Mississippi, won three straight national titles from 1975 to 1977. Lusia Harris, who averaged 25.9 points and 14.4 rebounds throughout college, led the way. She later became the first women's college basketball player and the first Black woman to be enshrined in the Basketball Hall of Fame.

With women's basketball growing in popularity, the NCAA began sponsoring the sport in 1981–82. Some schools still valued the AIAW since it was run by women and prioritized the interests of female athletes. However, the NCAA offered many perks, including paying for transportation to tournament games. As a result, most of the top women's basketball programs left the AIAW to join the NCAA.

Delta State (dark uniforms) and Louisiana State face off in the 1977 AIAW national championship game.

Forward Cheryl Miller (31) averaged 23.6 points and 12 rebounds per game during her career at USC in the early 1980s.

In March 1982, both the AIAW and the NCAA held national tournaments. Of the top 20 ranked teams heading into the postseason, 17 of them played in the NCAA Tournament. Both championship games took place on March 28.

Louisiana Tech, the 1981 AIAW champion, defeated Cheyney State to win the first NCAA title in front of a nationally televised audience. Meanwhile, Rutgers took down Texas to win the AIAW championship in a game that wasn't broadcast on TV. After the 1981–82 season, the AIAW folded.

## BATTLE OF THE DYNASTIES

Thirty-six teams from around the country took part in the 1983 NCAA Tournament. That marked the beginning of University of Southern California (USC) forward Cheryl Miller taking over the sport. The freshman star led the Trojans to a win over Louisiana Tech for their first national title in 1983. Then Miller's USC team beat Tennessee to win another one in 1984.

The 1984 tournament marked the third time Tennessee had lost in a title game under coach Pat Summitt. But she'd soon turn the Lady Volunteers into a force. Tennessee won its first national title in 1987, and by 1991 the team had won two more.

The Lady Volunteers made it back to the championship game in 1995, which was the second year with a 64-team tournament. Tennessee faced off against an up-and-coming Connecticut Huskies team that was playing in its first national title game under coach Geno Auriemma. And when the team known as UConn won, a rivalry began that would define the sport for years to come.

Tennessee coach Pat Summitt, *left*, and UConn coach Geno Auriemma built up the sport's iconic rivalry.

Over the next 15 years, UConn and Tennessee won a combined total of 11 national championships. Ultimately, Summitt and Auriemma coached against each other 21 times, with six of those matchups coming in the NCAA Tournament. Tennessee beat UConn on the way to championships in 1996 and 1997. The rivals met again in the 2000, 2003, and 2004 national title games, with the Huskies winning all three.

## NEW CONTENDERS

By the early 2010s, UConn was firmly established as the sport's dominant program. From 2013 to 2016, the Huskies won four national titles in a row while losing only five games. Some other

## HISTORIC UPSET

Stanford coach Tara VanDerveer led her program to two national titles and six Final Four appearances during the 1990s. The Cardinal appeared poised for another deep run in 1998 as a No. 1 seed. Instead, No. 16 Harvard took a 66–65 lead with 1:34 remaining in their opening-round matchup. The Crimson went on to stun the Cardinal 71–67. They became the first No. 16 seed to upset a No. 1 seed in the women's or men's NCAA Tournament.

teams emerged as powers during this decade too. Coach Kim Mulkey led Baylor to its first national title in 2005, and her team added two more in the 2010s.

Baylor's latter two championships came over Notre Dame. The Fighting Irish made several deep runs in the tournament

Baylor players celebrate after winning the 2019 NCAA championship.

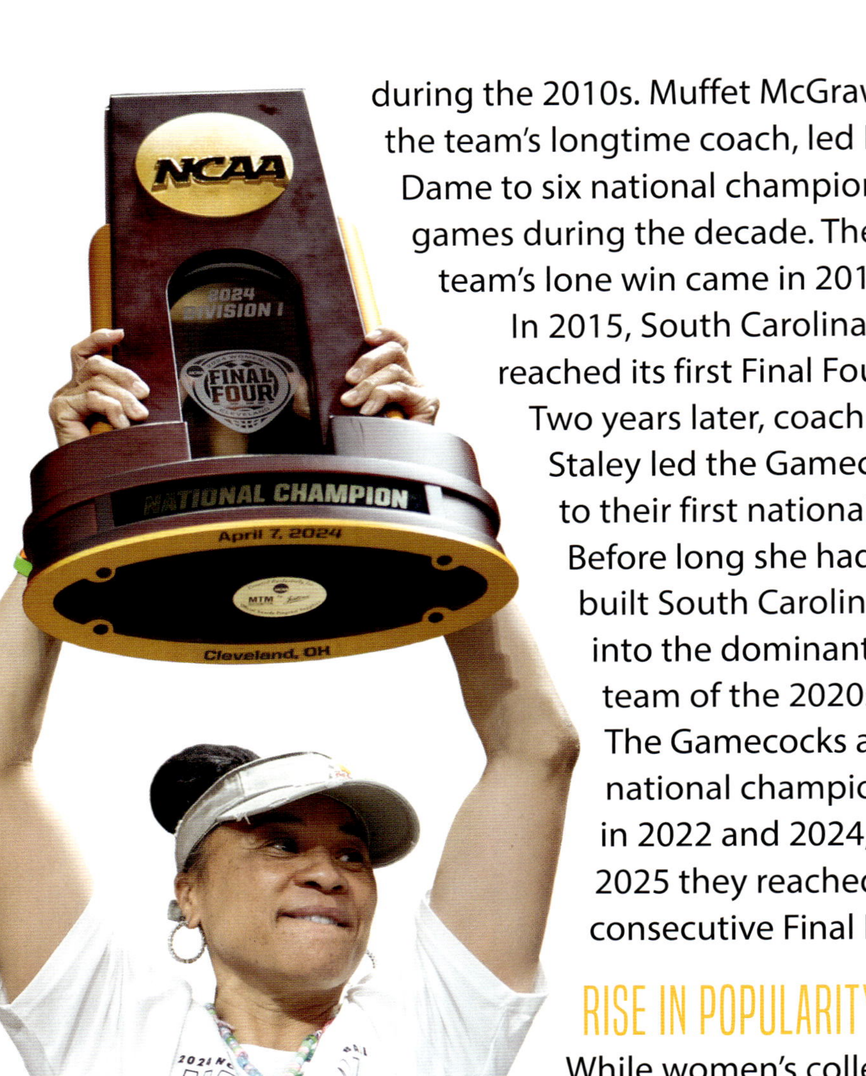


during the 2010s. Muffet McGraw, the team's longtime coach, led Notre Dame to six national championship games during the decade. The team's lone win came in 2018. In 2015, South Carolina reached its first Final Four. Two years later, coach Dawn Staley led the Gamecocks to their first national title. Before long she had built South Carolina into the dominant team of the 2020s. The Gamecocks added national championships in 2022 and 2024, and in 2025 they reached a fifth consecutive Final Four.

## RISE IN POPULARITY

While women's college basketball had steadily grown since the 1970s, the sport trailed men's

South Carolina coach Dawn Staley lifts the NCAA championship trophy in 2024. The title was the Gamecocks' third in eight years.

Iowa guard Caitlin Clark made 548 three-pointers from 2020 to 2024, the most in women's college basketball history.

basketball in terms of investment and popularity. By the 2020s, however, interest in the women's game became impossible to ignore. This coincided with new rules established in July 2021 that allowed college athletes to earn money off their name, image, and likeness (NIL). Previously, college athletes were not allowed to earn money while in school.

No one defined this new era quite like Iowa guard Caitlin Clark. With her deep step-back three-pointers and crisp passing skills, Clark electrified arenas. Her incredible play helped the Hawkeyes reach back-to-back national title games in 2023 and 2024. And unlike stars who had come before, she gained extra exposure from appearing in commercials for brands such as Gatorade and State Farm.

The 2023 national title game was Iowa's first. A women's record 9.9 million viewers tuned in to watch the Hawkeyes take on Louisiana State (LSU) and its superstar forward, Angel Reese. The Tigers, then coached by Mulkey, won the game to

## MARCH MADNESS

The men's NCAA Tournament has long been nicknamed "March Madness." However, for many years the NCAA didn't let the women's tournament use the nickname. That finally changed in 2022. The decision was one of many around that time meant to address inequities between the men's and women's game at the college level.

clinch their first title. A year later, the teams met again in the Elite Eight. The rematch lived up to the hype, with Clark scoring 41 points to lead Iowa back to the Final Four. With an average TV audience of 12.3 million people, that game became the most-watched in women's college basketball history.

The record kept falling as Iowa advanced in the tournament. An average audience of more than 14 million viewers tuned in to watch Iowa defeat UConn and its star guard, Paige Bueckers, in the Final Four. Then 18.7 million people watched as South Carolina finished an undefeated season by beating Iowa in the national championship game. It marked the first time that more people tuned in for the women's basketball title game than the men's.

Clark was hardly the only star to emerge during this era. Reese developed a huge following of her own. And even after they graduated in 2024, stars such as Bueckers, USC's JuJu Watkins, and LSU's Flau'jae Johnson continued to drive high viewership numbers. Meanwhile, the NCAA continues to invest in the women's game, giving fans reason to believe the sport's best days are yet to come.

USC guard JuJu Watkins (12) dribbles past UConn guard Paige Bueckers during a game in December 2024.

# ARIZONA WILDCATS

In 2003–04, Joan Bonvicini, *left*, coached Arizona to a share of the Pac-10 Conference regular-season title for the first time in program history.

The Arizona Wildcats began playing in 1972–73 and mostly struggled in their early years. In the program's first 19 seasons, Arizona went through six coaches. Those coaches led the team to only four winning seasons. Joan Bonvicini was hired in 1991 to change the Wildcats' fortunes.

The turnaround didn't happen right away. But by 1997, Bonvicini led Arizona to its first NCAA Tournament appearance. A year later, senior forward Adia Barnes led the Pacific-10 Conference with 21.8 points per game. Then she put up 30 points against Virginia in the NCAA Tournament to send the Wildcats on to their first Sweet 16.

That proved to be the tournament high point for the Wildcats under Bonvicini, who was fired in 2008 following three straight losing seasons. By 2016, the team was still looking for a breakthrough. So Arizona brought Barnes back, this time to coach the team.

By 2019–20, the Wildcats were a top-ten team. However, the NCAA Tournament was canceled that year due to the COVID-19 pandemic. One year later, senior guard Aari McDonald led the Wildcats to their best season ever. Standing only 5 feet, 6 inches tall, McDonald used her quick dribbling to zoom past

Wildcats coach Adia Barnes celebrates advancing to the 2021 Final Four.

defenders and score. And she was at her best in the NCAA Tournament.

Arizona entered the 2021 tournament as a No. 3 seed. Behind McDonald, the Wildcats went on a tear. The senior star scored 31 points in a win over No. 2 Texas A&M in the Sweet 16. She bettered that in the Elite Eight by dropping 33 points in a win over No. 4 Indiana.

## A FIRST STEP

Before coach Adia Barnes led Arizona back to the NCAA Tournament, her Wildcats played in the 2019 Women's National Invitation Tournament (WNIT). The team won five games to reach the WNIT championship game. Hosting Northwestern in front of a program-record crowd of 14,644, Arizona won 56–42. Sophomore guard Aari McDonald scored a team-high 19 points and added six steals in the win.

Arizona guard Aari McDonald averaged 24.8 points per game during the 2021 NCAA Tournament.

That set up a Final Four meeting with top-seeded Connecticut. Huskies guard Paige Bueckers won that year's Naismith Award as the national player of the year. In the national semifinal, however, it was McDonald who stole the show. She scored a game-high 26 points to send the Wildcats to the national final with a 69–59 victory.

In the national title game, Arizona faced Pac-12 rival Stanford, which had defeated the Wildcats twice in the regular season. Their third meeting came down to the very end. With six seconds left, Arizona had the ball trailing 54–53. However, McDonald's last-second jumper clanked off the rim to end the team's title hopes.

## FACT BOX

**First Season:** 1972–73

**Location:** Tucson, Arizona

**Arena:** McKale Center

**Conference:** Big 12 Conference

**All-Time Record:** 626–647

**NCAA Tournament Appearances:** 11

**Final Fours:** 1

**National Titles:** None

**Top Coaches:** Joan Bonvicini (1992–2008); Adia Barnes (2016– )

**Top Players:** Adia Barnes (1994–98); Dee-Dee Wheeler (2001–05); Shawntinice Polk (2002–05); Ify Ibekwe (2007–11); Davellyn Whyte (2009–13); Aari McDonald (2018–21)

**Mascot:** Wilma T. Wildcat

Auburn had already enjoyed some success by the time it hired coach Joe Ciampi in 1979. The team, founded in 1971–72, finished with a winning record in each of its first six seasons. Under Ciampi, however, the Tigers became one of the nation's top programs.

Ciampi led the Tigers to the inaugural NCAA Tournament in 1982. Though they fell in the first round that year, the Tigers advanced to the Sweet 16 the next year. Soon, making the tournament became routine under Ciampi.

Behind All-America sophomore center Vickie Orr, Auburn earned its first No. 1 seed in 1987. The Tigers made a run to the Elite Eight before losing to eventual national champion Tennessee. The Tigers then made three straight trips to the

Auburn coach Joe Ciampi, *left*, celebrates as the Tigers defeat Louisiana Tech in the 1989 Final Four.

Guard Carolyn Young averaged 18.3 points per game during her Auburn career from 1988 to 1991.

national title game from 1988 to 1990. No team had achieved that in the NCAA era.

The top-ranked Tigers rolled into the 1988 tournament with a 28–2 record and then won four games to reach the national title game. A big first half by junior guard Ruthie Bolton helped Auburn build a 31–19 lead over Louisiana Tech. However, the powerful Lady Techsters battled back to win 56–54.

The Tigers got revenge against Louisiana Tech in the 1989 Final Four. Orr poured in 18 points in a 76–71 Auburn win. However, this time the Tigers fell to Tennessee in the title game. Auburn beat Louisiana Tech again in the 1990 Final Four.

That set up a title-game showdown against Stanford. Despite junior guard Carolyn Young scoring a game-high 24 points, Auburn missed out on the championship again, losing 88–81.

Ciampi coached Auburn through the 2003–04 season. While he never led the Tigers to an NCAA title, the team did win a WNIT championship in 2003. Once Ciampi left, the Tigers struggled to find consistency. One highlight came in 2008–09. That season, All-America senior forward DeWanna Bonner was named Southeastern Conference (SEC) Player of the Year after leading the Tigers to their first conference title in 20 years.

Auburn forward DeWanna Bonner led the SEC in scoring in 2008–09 with 21.1 points per game.

## RUTHIE BOLTON

In the 1988 Final Four, Auburn trailed Long Beach State early in the fourth quarter. Then junior guard Ruthie Bolton exploded for 11 points in the game's final six minutes. Her performance led Auburn to a 68–55 win and a spot in its first national title game. One year later, she helped the Tigers get back there. During Bolton's four college seasons, the Tigers had a record of 119–13. She later won two Olympic gold medals with Team USA.

## FACT BOX

**First Season:** 1971–72

**Location:** Auburn, Alabama

**Arena:** Neville Arena

**Conference:** Southeastern Conference

**All-Time Record:** 1,007–579

**NCAA Tournament Appearances:** 22

**Final Fours:** 3

**National Titles:** None

**Top Coaches:** Joe Ciampi (1979–2004); Nell Fortner (2004–12)

**Top Players:** Becky Jackson (1980–84); Ruthie Bolton (1985–89); Vickie Orr (1985–89); Carolyn Young (1987–91); Lauretta Freeman (1989–93); Natasha Brackett (2001–05); DeWanna Bonner (2005–09); Unique Thompson (2017–21)

**Mascot:** Aubie the Tiger

# BAYLOR BEARS

When Baylor created its women's basketball team in 1974–75, the school knew whom to call to be the coach. Olga Fallen also led the Texas school's softball and women's track-and-field teams. Basketball proved to be a good fit too. The Bears won at least 30 games in each of their first four seasons. However, Fallen left after a 17–13 finish in 1978–79. For the next two decades, the team struggled to match the success of its first few seasons.

That finally changed in 2000–01, when Kim Mulkey came in as coach. Known for her fiery coaching style and suffocating defense, Mulkey led the Bears to their first NCAA Tournament appearance that season. Behind junior forward Sophia Young, the Bears won their first Big 12 Conference title in 2004–05. Young then put up a game-high 26 points to help Baylor beat

Hall of Fame coach Kim Mulkey led Baylor to new heights during her time leading the program from 2000 to 2021.

## SERIAL WINNER

Kim Mulkey played at Louisiana Tech from 1980 to 1984. She helped the Lady Techsters win the AIAW title in 1981 and the NCAA championship in 1982. Mulkey made history when she led Baylor to its first national title in 2005. That made her the first woman to win a college basketball championship as a player and a coach.

Michigan State 84–62 and claim the team's first national championship.

Two Texas natives soon had the Bears back on top. Houston native Brittney Griner arrived in 2009–10. The towering 6-foot-8-inch center averaged 6.4 blocks per game as a freshman and led the Bears to the Final Four. Odyssey Sims joined

Baylor center Brittney Griner (42) set an NCAA record with 748 blocks from 2009 to 2013.

Baylor guard Chloe Jackson scores the game-winning layup in the 2019 NCAA championship game.

Griner the next season. The point guard from Irving, Texas, shut down opposing guards. By 2011–12, the duo couldn't be beat. The Bears rolled into the NCAA Tournament with a 34–0 record. Once there, they won all six of their games by at least 12 points to cap off a perfect season with a national title.

Under Mulkey, Baylor continued to make deep runs in the tournament. Her 2018–19 squad featured seven players who later went on to the Women's National Basketball Association (WNBA). The Bears made a run to the national title game that year. Guard Chloe Jackson buried a layup in the game's final seconds to put Baylor up for good in an 82–81 win over Notre Dame.

After the 2020–21 season, Mulkey left Baylor. In her 21 seasons, the Bears won three national championships and twelve Big 12 titles. Nicki Collen took over in 2021–22 and led Baylor to its twelfth straight conference championship.

## FACT BOX

**First Season:** 1974–75

**Location:** Waco, Texas

**Arena:** Foster Pavilion

**Conference:** Big 12 Conference

**All-Time Record:** 1,128–538

**NCAA Tournament Appearances:** 23

**Final Fours:** 4

**National Titles:** 2005, 2012, 2019

**Top Coaches:** Kim Mulkey (2000–21); Nicki Collen (2021– )

**Top Players:** Sophia Young (2002–06); Brittney Griner (2009–13); Odyssey Sims (2010–14); Nina Davis (2013–17); Kalani Brown (2015–19); Lauren Cox (2016–20); NaLyssa Smith (2018–22)

**Mascot:** Marigold

The Connecticut Huskies, also known as UConn, played their first season in 1974–75. The team finished with a winning season just once in its first ten seasons. Then, in 1985, Geno Auriemma took over as coach. He eventually turned the program into the sport's most successful dynasty.

UConn officially arrived as a national power in 1994–95. With a loaded roster highlighted by star forward Rebecca Lobo, the Huskies finished the regular season undefeated and made a run to the national championship game. Their opponent, Tennessee, had won three championships since 1987. But UConn held on to win 70–64 and secure the program's first national title. The win also made the Huskies only the second team in the NCAA era to finish a season as undefeated national champions.

Since taking over in 1985, Geno Auriemma has built UConn into the sport's most successful program.

In the 2000s, UConn regularly boasted some of the best players in the country. Point guard Sue Bird's crisp passing helped the Huskies win national titles in 2000 and 2002. After Bird won the Naismith Award in 2002, sharpshooting guard Diana Taurasi won the award in 2003 and 2004. The Huskies won national titles both years.

The dynamic duo of forward Maya Moore and center Tina Charles took over later in the decade. UConn finished off perfect seasons in 2008–09 and 2009–10 with national titles. Moore won her first Naismith Award in 2009, while Charles took home the award in 2010.

In 2012–13, freshman forward Breanna Stewart served as a defensive anchor to help UConn win its eighth national title. Over the next three seasons, she developed into a go-to scorer for the Huskies and won three straight Naismith Awards. In her four years at UConn, Stewart won four national championships and led the team to a 151–5 record.

The Huskies went 150–4 with guard Maya Moore from 2007 to 2011.

UConn then went eight seasons without another national title. It was the longest gap between titles since the first one. Paige Bueckers finally put an end to the drought. The star guard scored 17 points in an 82–59 rout of South Carolina in the 2025 title game.

In 2016, UConn forward Breanna Stewart won her third Naismith Award. That made her only the second player to win the award three times.

## ALL THEY DO IS WIN

On November 17, 2014, Stanford defeated UConn in double overtime to end the Huskies' 47-game winning streak. Six days later, the Huskies smashed Creighton 96–60 and began a new streak. This one wouldn't end for more than two years. UConn won 111 games in a row, securing two national titles in the process. Mississippi State finally defeated the Huskies 66–64 in overtime on March 31, 2017, to end the longest winning streak in college basketball history.

## FACT BOX

**First Season:** 1974–75

**Location:** Storrs, Connecticut

**Arena:** Harry A. Gampel Pavilion

**Conference:** Big East Conference

**All-Time Record:** 1,341–327

**NCAA Tournament Appearances:** 36

**Final Fours:** 24

**National Titles:** 1995, 2000, 2002, 2003, 2004, 2009, 2010, 2013, 2014, 2015, 2016, 2025

**Top Coaches:** Geno Auriemma (1985– )

**Top Players:** Rebecca Lobo (1991–95); Sue Bird (1998–2002); Diana Taurasi (2000–04); Tina Charles (2006–10); Maya Moore (2007–11); Breanna Stewart (2012–16); Napheesa Collier (2015–19); Paige Bueckers (2020–25)

**Mascot:** Jonathan the Husky

# UCONN DYNASTY

Led by coach Geno Auriemma, UConn won its first national title in 1995. By 2013, the Huskies had won eight. That tied them with Tennessee for the most in the sport's history. Then UConn charged to the record by winning again in 2014, 2015, and 2016. Following eight seasons without a title, the team won its record-extending twelfth championship in 2025. Tennessee remained second with eight wins. No other school had more than three.

All-America center Rebecca Lobo led UConn past Tennessee in the 1995 NCAA title game.

Star guard Paige Bueckers played in three Final Fours before finally leading the Huskies back to the top in her fourth try in 2025.

# DUKE BLUE DEVILS

Duke often struggled in its early years, starting in 1972–73. Joining the tough Atlantic Coast Conference (ACC) in 1982 didn't help. But then, in 1986–87, forward Chris Moreland helped the Blue Devils break through. Behind her 20.9 points per game, Duke finally reached its first NCAA Tournament.

The Blue Devils needed more time to become consistent winners. Gail Goestenkors became coach in 1992–93. By her third season, Duke was back in the NCAA Tournament. In 1997–98, the team won its first ACC title. That year also marked the team's first run to the Elite Eight.

Duke was back in the Elite Eight in 1999. This time, the Blue Devils faced the three-time defending national champion Tennessee Lady Volunteers. In a massive upset, Duke won 69–63 to reach its first Final Four. Then Michele Van Gorp and Nicole Erickson scored a combined total of 42 points to take down

Starting in 2001–02, Duke guard Alana Beard led the ACC in scoring for three straight seasons.

Duke coach Gail Goestenkors, *right*, gives instructions to guard Lindsey Harding during a 2006 game.

Georgia 81–69. Duke's magical run came to an end in the title game, though, as Purdue won 62–45.

Duke continued to have success under Goestenkors. In 2002, sophomore guard Alana Beard earned All-America honors for her elite two-way play. In that year's NCAA Tournament, Beard averaged 21.8 points per game and lifted the Blue Devils back to the Final Four. But they lost to Oklahoma there.

Four years later, Duke made another deep run. The Blue Devils routed LSU in the Final Four to set up a title-game

## SHOT STOPPER

Elizabeth Williams set the standard for defenders during her four years at Duke. The England-born center arrived in 2011–12. Standing 6 feet, 3 inches tall, she led the ACC in blocks all four of her seasons. The conference named her its Defensive Player of the Year all four years as well.

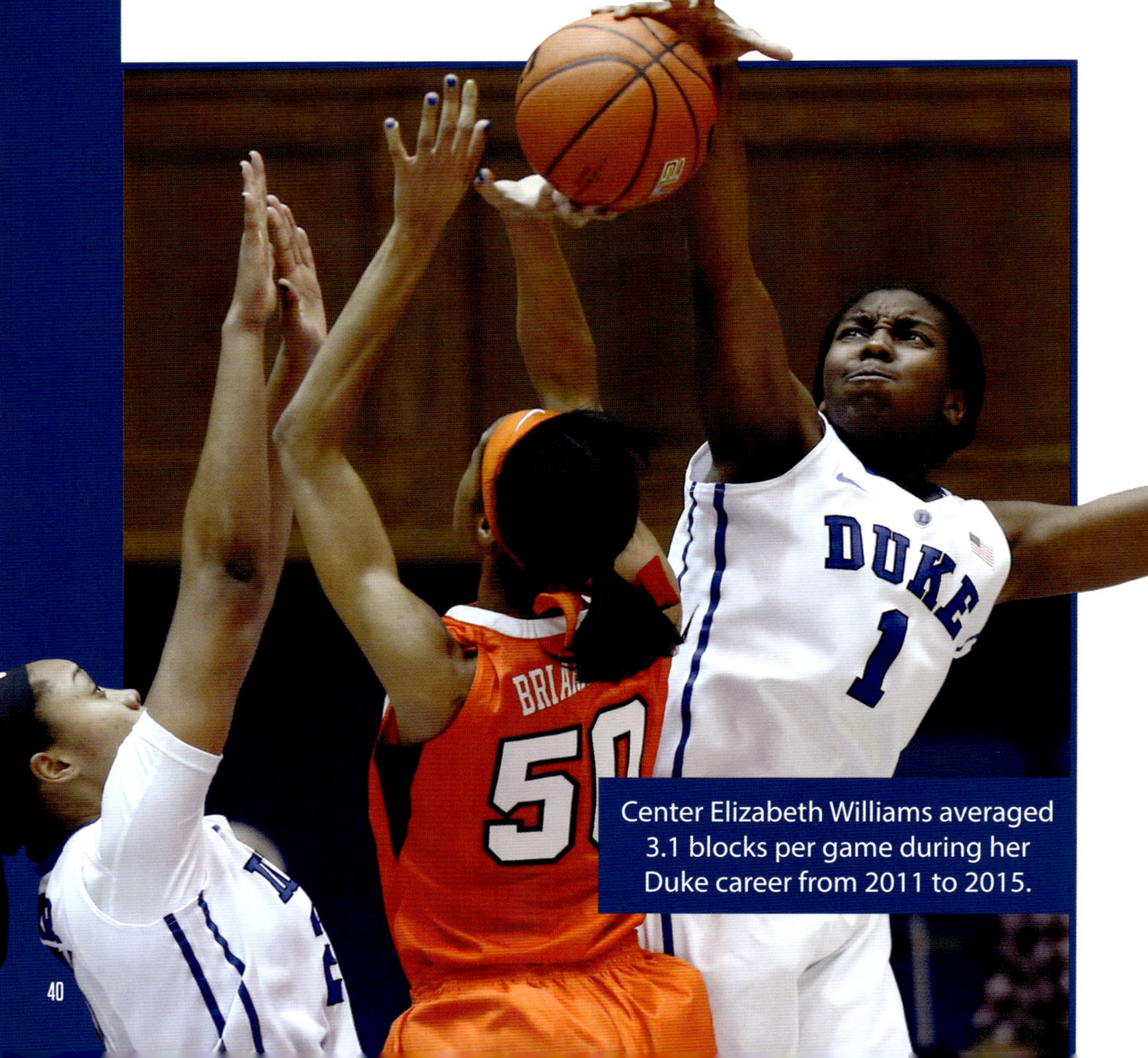


Center Elizabeth Williams averaged 3.1 blocks per game during her Duke career from 2011 to 2015.

showdown with ACC rival Maryland. The game was tied 70–70 with only six seconds to play. Duke raced up the court. Guard Lindsey Harding got a shot off before the buzzer sounded, but it clanked off the rim. Maryland went on to win 78–75 in overtime.

A year later, Harding won the Naismith Award after carrying Duke to a 32–2 record. But Rutgers upset Duke in the Sweet 16. Goestenkors then left Duke after 15 seasons. A new era of success began in 2020, when Kara Lawson took over as coach. Her teams became a defensive force. In 2025, Duke returned to the Elite Eight for the first time in 12 years.

## FACT BOX

**First Season:** 1972–73

**Location:** Durham, North Carolina

**Arena:** Cameron Indoor Stadium

**Conference:** Atlantic Coast Conference

**All-Time Record:** 1,037–463

**NCAA Tournament Appearances:** 27

**Final Fours:** 4

**National Titles:** None

**Top Coaches:** Gail Goestenkors (1992–2007); Joanne Palombo-McCallie (2007–20); Kara Lawson (2020– )

**Top Players:** Chris Moreland (1984–88); Alana Beard (2000–04); Monique Currie (2001–06); Lindsey Harding (2002–07); Chelsea Gray (2010–14); Elizabeth Williams (2011–15)

**Mascot:** The Blue Devil

# GEORGIA LADY BULLDOGS

Over Georgia's first six seasons, the Lady Bulldogs had only one winning record. Coach Andy Landers took over the struggling program in 1979. Before long, winning seasons became routine for Georgia.

Freshman forward Janet Harris averaged 22.4 points and 12.4 rebounds per game in 1981–82. Her stellar play helped Georgia make the inaugural NCAA Tournament. One year later, guard Teresa Edwards partnered with Harris to lift the Lady Bulldogs to the SEC Tournament title. Then Georgia upset conference rival Tennessee 67–63 in the Elite Eight.

Two years later, the Lady Bulldogs got back to the Final Four. The 1985 national semifinal against Western Kentucky turned into a fast-paced game. Edwards scored a game-high 29 points, while sophomore center Katrina McClain added 25. Their scoring outburst led Georgia to a 91–78 win.

Georgia's Andy Landers earned SEC Coach of the Year honors in 1984, 1991, and 1996.

The Lady Bulldogs faced Old Dominion in the championship game. However, both Edwards and McClain fouled out. The Lady Bulldogs couldn't overcome the loss of their stars and fell 70–65.

Georgia remained one of the top teams in the SEC for several years. In 1995 and 1996, the Lady Bulldogs got back to the Final Four. Tennessee ended their first run. The next year, Georgia senior guard Saudia Roundtree stepped up. The Naismith Award winner put up 26 points in a win over Stanford. However, Tennessee was waiting in the national title game, and the powerful Lady Volunteers beat the Lady Bulldogs 83–65.

Lady Bulldogs guard Saudia Roundtree led the SEC in assists in 1994–95 and 1995–96.

## A LATE RUN

Georgia trailed top-seeded Colorado by 10 points with less than five minutes to play in the 1995 Elite Eight. That's when Kedra Holland came alive. The guard drained three three-pointers to get Georgia back in the game. The Lady Bulldogs eventually beat the Buffaloes 82–79.

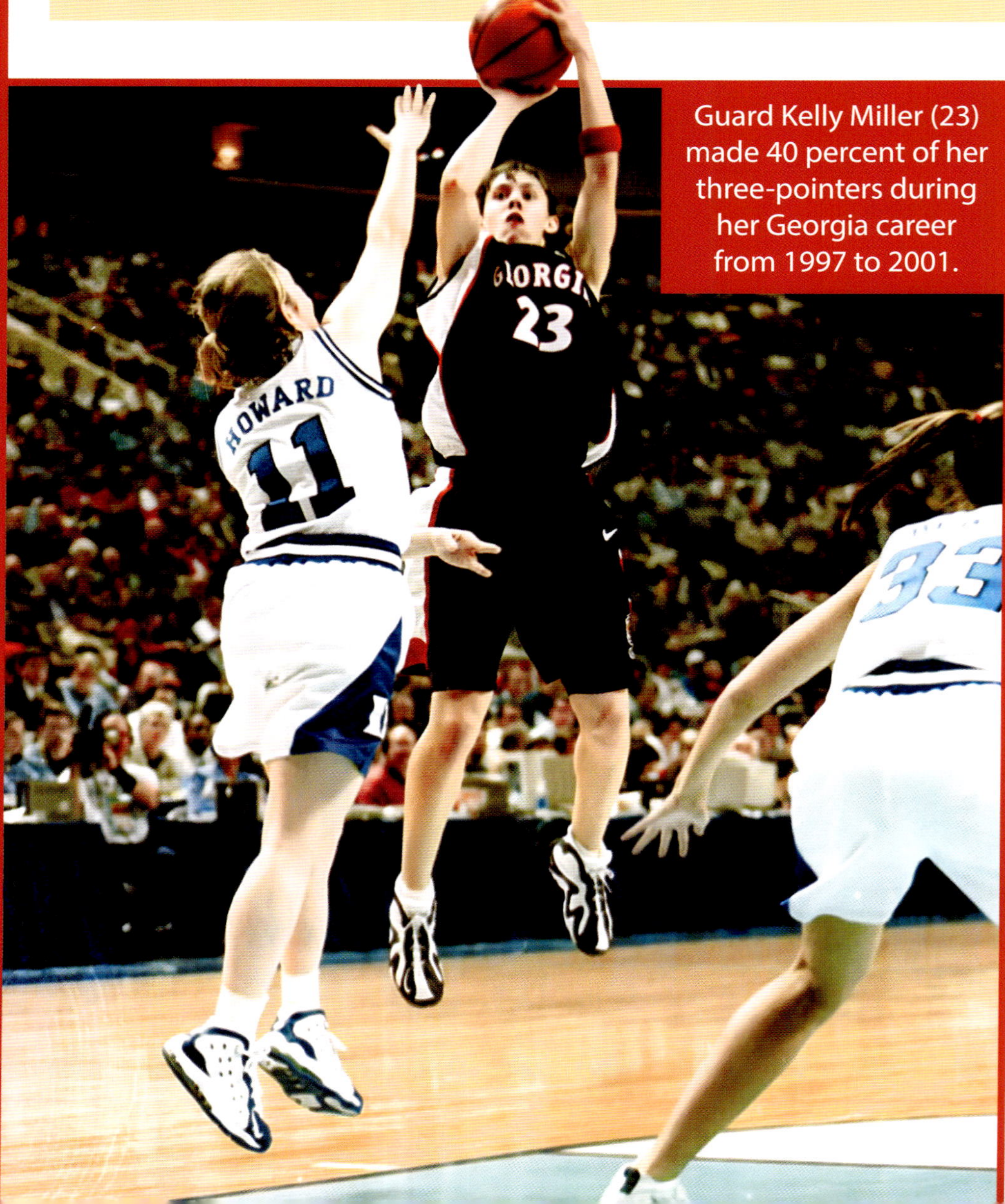


Guard Kelly Miller (23) made 40 percent of her three-pointers during her Georgia career from 1997 to 2001.

Identical twin sisters Coco and Kelly Miller were the top two scorers for the Lady Bulldogs in 1998–99. In an Elite Eight game against Iowa State, Kelly drained six three-pointers and finished with 33 points. Coco added 16 points to send the Lady Bulldogs to the Final Four. However, they fell to Duke 81–69.

In 2015, Georgia fell short of the NCAA Tournament. That snapped a streak of 20 straight tournament berths under Landers. The coach left after that. In the next ten years, Georgia made only five NCAA Tournaments and never got past the second round.

## FACT BOX

**First Season:** 1973–74

**Location:** Athens, Georgia

**Arena:** Stegeman Coliseum

**Conference:** Southeastern Conference

**All-Time Record:** 1,086–508

**NCAA Tournament Appearances:** 36

**Final Fours:** 5

**National Titles:** None

**Top Coaches:** Andy Landers (1979–2015)

**Top Players:** Janet Harris (1981–85); Teresa Edwards (1982–86); Katrina McClain (1983–87); La'Keshia Frett (1993–97); Saudia Roundtree (1994–96); Coco Miller (1997–2001); Kelly Miller (1997–2001); Tasha Humphrey (2004–08)

**Mascot:** Hairy Dawg

# GREEN BAY PHOENIX

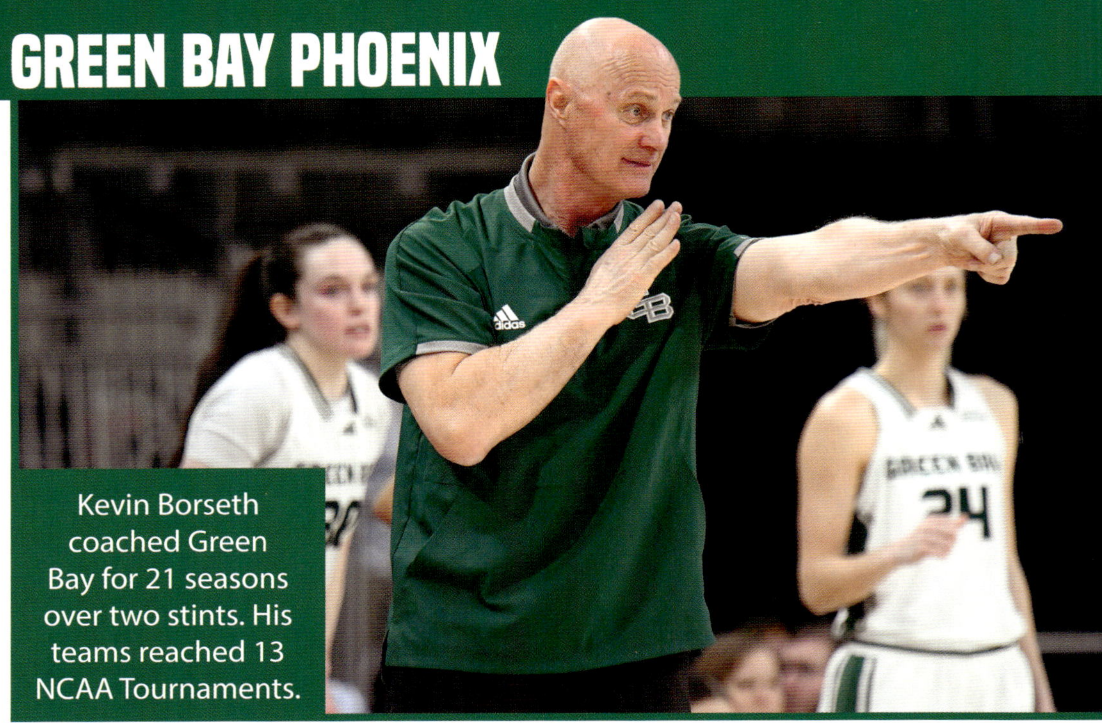


Kevin Borseth coached Green Bay for 21 seasons over two stints. His teams reached 13 NCAA Tournaments.

Carol Hammerle coached Green Bay for its first 25 seasons. The team underwent a lot of changes during that time. Established in 1973 as a Division II program, Green Bay moved to Division I in 1987. The team spent time as an independent and as part of the Mid-Continent Conference. Since 1995, it's played in what's now called the Horizon League.

One thing didn't change much under Hammerle. Green Bay was a consistently winning team. By the time she left for a new job in 1998, the Phoenix had won 456 games and reached the NCAA Tournament twice.

New coach Kevin Borseth kept the winning going. The Phoenix won their conference tournament in six of his first seven years. In 2003, Green Bay opened the NCAA Tournament against Washington. Five Phoenix players scored at least

10 points as the program clinched its first tournament win. The Phoenix returned to the tournament in three of the next four seasons, winning another first-round game in 2007.

Borseth left after that. New coach Matt Bollant kept Green Bay a regular in the tournament. His 2010–11 squad won a school-record 34 games. In the NCAA Tournament, No. 5 seed Green Bay took down Little Rock and Michigan State to reach the Sweet 16 for the first time. Facing No. 1 seed Baylor, guards Kayla Tetschlag and Celeste Hoewisch combined to score 47 points. However, it wasn't enough as the Bears won 86–76.

Bollant coached Green Bay to another win in the NCAA Tournament in 2012. After that season, he took another job

Green Bay's Kayla Tetschlag (42) and Julie Wojta (32) celebrate a first-round win in the 2011 NCAA Tournament.

Green Bay guard Celeste Hoewisch was named the 2010–11 Horizon League Player of the Year.

## TOURNEY TIME

Senior center Kim Wood anchored Green Bay's defense during the 1993–94 season. She helped the Phoenix defeat Northern Illinois in the conference title game. That earned the team a spot in its first NCAA Tournament. However, Stanford took down Green Bay 81–56.

and Borseth came back to Green Bay. Over the next 12 seasons, he led the Phoenix back to the NCAA Tournament six times. That included a trip in 2024, which was Green Bay's 38th winning season in a row. Only Tennessee had a longer streak of winning seasons.

Borseth retired after the 2023–24 season. Green Bay hired former star player Tetschlag to continue its winning tradition. In her first season as coach, the Phoenix extended their streak of winning seasons while returning to the NCAA Tournament.

## FACT BOX

**First Season:** 1973–74

**Location:** Green Bay, Wisconsin

**Arena:** Kress Events Center

**Conference:** Horizon League

**All-Time Record:** 1,142–397

**NCAA Tournament Appearances:** 20

**Final Fours:** None

**National Titles:** None

**Top Coaches:** Carol Hammerle (1973–98); Kevin Borseth (1998–2007, 2012–24)

**Top Players:** Kim Wood (1990–94); Chari Nordgaard (1995–99); Nicole Soulis (2003–07); Celeste Hoewisch (2007–11); Kayla Tetschlag (2007–11); Julie Wojta (2008–12); Mehryn Kraker (2013–17)

**Mascot:** The Phoenix

# IOWA HAWKEYES

The Iowa Hawkeyes were a mostly losing team from their start in 1974 until 1983, when C. Vivian Stringer took over as coach. In 1986, the Hawkeyes reached their first NCAA Tournament. That began a streak of nine straight appearances.

As a No. 1 seed, Iowa reached the 1988 Elite Eight. The Hawkeyes earned a No. 1 seed again in 1992. However, this time they were upset by Missouri State in the second round. Iowa finally broke through to the Final Four the next year as a No. 2 seed. Behind a stout defense and Big Ten Player of the

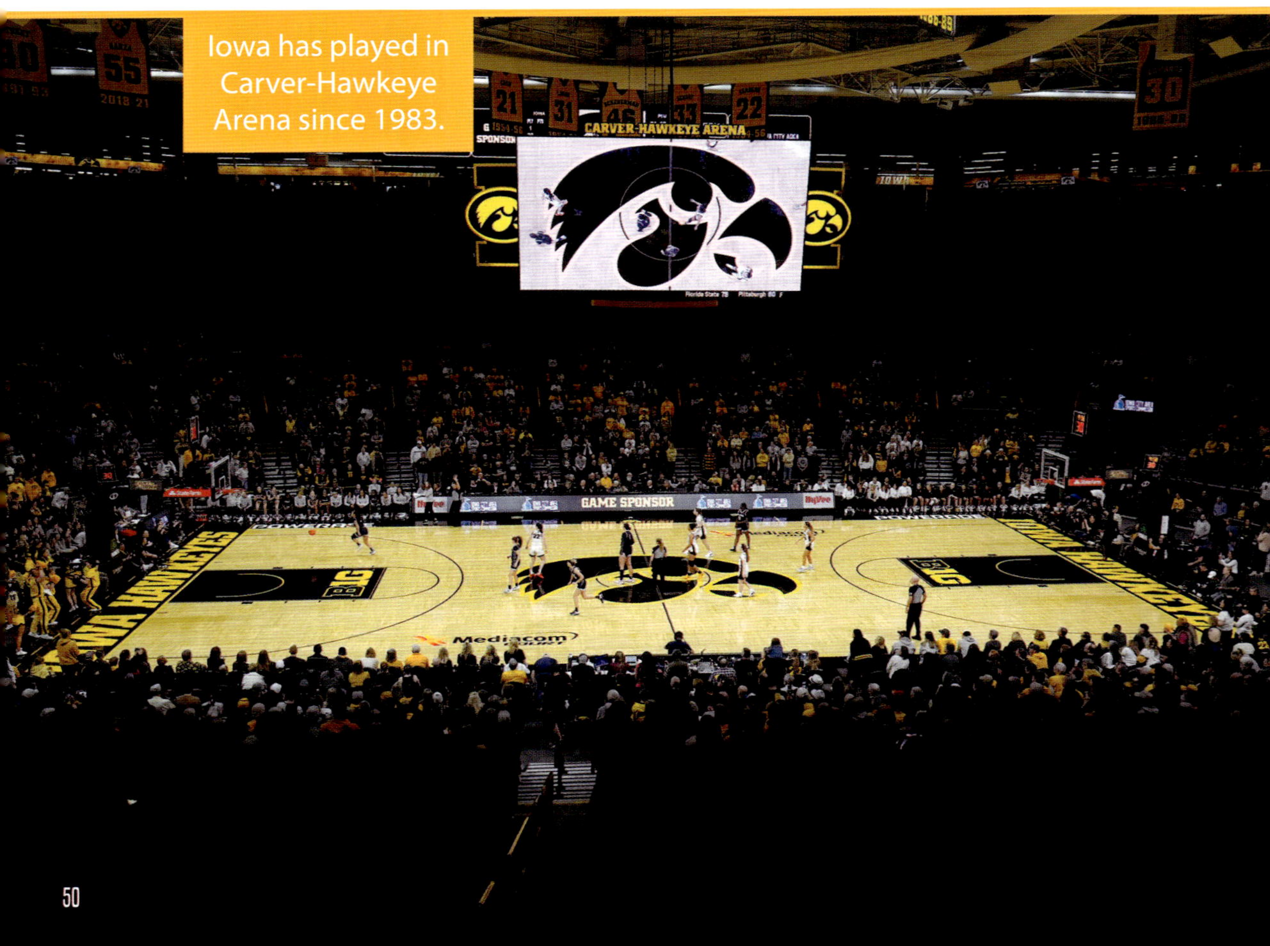


Iowa has played in Carver-Hawkeye Arena since 1983.

Year Toni Foster, Iowa upset Tennessee 72–56 in the Elite Eight. The Hawkeyes nearly won their next game too. They fell 73–72 in overtime to Big Ten rival Ohio State.

A new period of success began when Lisa Bluder took over as Iowa's coach in 2000. The Hawkeyes became regulars in the NCAA Tournament. In 2017–18 and 2018–19, center Megan Gustafson led the nation in scoring. In the latter season, the senior star also earned the Naismith Award. Then, in the NCAA Tournament, Gustafson averaged 26 points and 14.3 rebounds per game as Iowa made a run to the 2019 Elite Eight.

Center Megan Gustafson averaged 20.8 points and 10.8 rebounds per game while at Iowa from 2015 to 2019.

Hawkeyes guard Caitlin Clark helped elevate college women's basketball with her huge scoring numbers from 2020 to 2024.

Two seasons later, Caitlin Clark lifted Iowa to an even higher level. The guard from Des Moines, Iowa, led the Big Ten in points and assists per game in each of her four seasons. Fans began to pack Carver-Hawkeye Arena to watch her play. Fans also filled arenas for Iowa road games.

## RECORD BREAKER

In February 2024, Caitlin Clark scored 33 points against Minnesota to pass Lynette Woodard as the leading scorer in women's college basketball history. Then, in March 2024, Clark established herself as the greatest scorer in college basketball history when she passed the men's record of 3,667 points, set by Pete Maravich. Clark finished her college career with 3,951 points.

Some of Clark's most memorable games came in the NCAA Tournament. In the 2023 Elite Eight, she recorded a triple-double in a win against Louisville. Then Clark scored 41 points to hand defending national champion South Carolina its first loss of the season. That win put Iowa in the national championship game for the first time.

LSU took down the Hawkeyes 102–85 in the 2023 title game. But Clark led Iowa back the next year. Clark, who won her second Naismith Award that season, scored 30 points in the championship game. However, it wasn't enough as Iowa fell to South Carolina 87–75.

## FACT BOX

**First Season:** 1974–75

**Location:** Iowa City, Iowa

**Arena:** Carver-Hawkeye Arena

**Conference:** Big Ten Conference

**All-Time Record:** 992–548

**NCAA Tournament Appearances:** 31

**Final Fours:** 3

**National Titles:** None

**Top Coaches:** C. Vivian Stringer (1983–95); Lisa Bluder (2000–24)

**Top Players:** Toni Foster (1989–93); Samantha Logic (2011–15); Megan Gustafson (2015–19); Kathleen Doyle (2016–20); Monika Czinano (2018–23); Caitlin Clark (2020–24)

**Mascot:** Herky the Hawk

# JAMES MADISON DUKES

James Madison's Duke Dog mascot debuted in 1982–83.

The James Madison Dukes played their first season in 1920–21. Few schools had women's basketball teams back then. Seasons often featured fewer than ten games. Nonetheless, the Dukes usually won more often than they lost.

By the 1980s, the sport was undergoing changes. James Madison hired coach Shelia Moorman in 1982 to lead the team into the new NCAA era. The Dukes clinched their first NCAA Tournament berth in 1986 after winning the Colonial Athletic Association (CAA) Tournament. As a No. 8 seed, James Madison beat No. 9 Providence 55–53 in the first round. Then Betsy Witman scored 19 points to lead the Dukes past No. 1

Virginia in a massive upset. Western Kentucky ended James Madison's run in the Sweet 16.

The Dukes continued to have success. They got back to the Sweet 16 in 1987 and 1988. In 1991, eighth-seeded James Madison met No. 1 Penn State in the second round. The Nittany Lions entered the game on an 18-game winning streak, and they led at halftime by 12. But a rousing halftime speech from Moorman inspired a comeback. The Dukes pulled off another huge upset, winning 73–71.

Kenny Brooks, *second from left*, celebrates winning his 303rd game at James Madison in 2015, making him the winningest coach in school history.

## UNDEFEATED

Althea Johnston began teaching at James Madison in 1909. The school later hired her to be its first women's basketball coach. Over her 22 seasons, the Dukes won 106 games. That included six undefeated seasons. Four other coaches led the Dukes to undefeated seasons from 1944–45 to 1956–57.

Moorman led the Dukes to one more NCAA Tournament in 1996 before moving into a new role with the school in 1997. By the time Kenny Brooks took over as coach during the 2002–03 season, James Madison had taken a step back in the CAA. Brooks soon changed that.

Under Brooks, James Madison won the

James Madison guard Kirby Burkholder averaged 24 points and 14 rebounds over two games in the 2014 NCAA Tournament.

CAA Tournament in 2007, 2010, and 2011. Each time, the Dukes lost in the first round of the NCAA Tournament. The team finally got past the first round in 2014. Senior guard Kirby Burkholder recorded 28 points and 18 rebounds as the No. 11 Dukes upset No. 6 Gonzaga 72–63. It marked James Madison's first tournament win since 1991.

Brooks coached the Dukes to two more CAA Tournament championships in 2015 and 2016. Then he left James Madison. The Dukes' next conference title came in 2023, when they won the Sun Belt during their first year in the conference.

## FACT BOX

**First Season:** 1920–21

**Location:** Harrisonburg, Virginia

**Arena:** Atlantic Union Bank Center

**Conference:** Sun Belt Conference

**All-Time Record:** 1,255–604

**NCAA Tournament Appearances:** 13

**Final Fours:** None

**National Titles:** None

**Top Coaches:** Althea Johnston (1920–42); Shelia Moorman (1982–97); Kenny Brooks (2002–16)

**Top Players:** Alisa Harris (1984–88); Sydney Beasley (1986–88); Meredith Alexis (2003–07); Dawn Evans (2007–11); Kirby Burkholder (2010–14); Precious Hall (2012–17); Kiki Jefferson (2019–23)

**Mascot:** Duke Dog

# KANSAS JAYHAWKS

Kansas guard Lynette Woodard was enshrined in the Basketball Hall of Fame in 2004.

The Jayhawks played their first season in 1968–69, and they joined the Big Eight Conference in 1975–76. However, the team didn't post a winning record until 1977–78. Lynette Woodard was a big reason why it finally did.

A 6-foot guard from nearby Wichita, Kansas, Woodard scored 833 points as a freshman in 1977–78. That set the school's scoring record. In a game against Kansas State that season, she grabbed a school-record 33 rebounds.

Woodard was even better as a sophomore. She shattered her own record by racking up 1,117 points. That remained a record through the 2024–25 season. In 1978–79, she led the Jayhawks to their first of three straight Big Eight titles. By the time she finished up at Kansas in 1981, Woodard

## COACH WASHINGTON

Marian Washington was just 26 years old when she began coaching the Jayhawks in 1973. Over 31 seasons, she led the team to 560 wins and 11 NCAA Tournaments. Washington was the first Black coach in Division I women's college basketball. She also served as the women's athletic director at Kansas and created its track-and-field team.

had scored 3,649 points. That stood as the women's college record until Iowa's Caitlin Clark broke it in 2024.

The Jayhawks made two NCAA Tournaments in the late 1980s. In 1992, they began a streak of nine straight berths. Kansas didn't get past the second round in the first four of those trips. In 1996, Kansas met Texas in the second round. Big Eight Player of the Year Tamecka Dixon scored 18 points. The Jayhawks' 77–70 win sent them to their first Sweet 16.

Marian Washington coached Kansas to six conference tournament titles from 1973 to 2004.

Kansas guard Angel Goodrich led the Big 12 in assists per game in 2010–11 and 2011–12.

Kansas's NCAA Tournament streak ended in 2001. The team didn't make it back until 2012. That year, the eleventh-seeded Jayhawks advanced all the way to the Sweet 16. The highlight was an upset win over No. 3 Delaware in the second round. Junior point guard Angel Goodrich scored 27 points and dished out six assists in the game.

One year later, Goodrich and the Jayhawks did it again. This time No. 12 seed Kansas upset fourth-seeded South Carolina in the second round. Goodrich scored 20 points with eight assists.

That proved to be the high point for a while. Kansas reached the tournament just twice in the next 12 years. And it never got past the second round.

## FACT BOX

**First Season:** 1968–69

**Location:** Lawrence, Kansas

**Arena:** Allen Fieldhouse

**Conference:** Big 12 Conference

**All-Time Record:** 926–732

**NCAA Tournament Appearances:** 15

**Final Fours:** None

**National Titles:** None

**Top Coaches:** Marian Washington (1973–2004)

**Top Players:** Adrian Mitchell (1975–79); Lynette Woodard (1977–81); Angela Aycock (1991–95); Tamecka Dixon (1993–97); Angel Goodrich (2009–13); Taiyanna Jackson (2021–24)

**Mascot:** Big Jay

# LOUISIANA STATE TIGERS

In only its second season, Louisiana State University (LSU) reached the 1977 AIAW championship game. However, the Tigers lost to Delta State. And they never reached another AIAW Tournament.

Guard Joyce Walker became a two-time All-American in the early 1980s. She led the Tigers to their first NCAA Tournament in 1984. That season was also Sue Gunter's second as LSU's coach. She turned the Tigers into regular contenders in the SEC.

LSU had reached the Elite Eight three times, including as a No. 1 seed in 2003. But heading into the 2004 NCAA Tournament, the Tigers had never reached a Final Four. Seimone Augustus helped change that trend. In 2004, the sophomore guard from Baton Rouge, Louisiana, poured in 29 points to take down conference rival Georgia in the Elite Eight. The Tigers nearly reached the championship game too.

Guard Seimone Augustus (33) earned All-America honors all four seasons at LSU, from 2002 to 2006.

However, Tennessee made a late basket to beat LSU 52–50.

Behind the high-scoring Augustus, LSU remained a power. The Tigers returned to the Final Four in 2005 and 2006. Augustus won the Naismith Award both seasons.

Sylvia Fowles kept LSU strong. The imposing center racked up blocks and rebounds. Behind her, LSU got back to the Final Four in 2007 and 2008. The Tigers got within one score of the national title game in 2008. However, just as in 2004, Tennessee hit a late game-winning shot. This time the Lady Volunteers scored with 0.7 seconds left.

Center Sylvia Fowles (34) left LSU in 2008 with 1,570 rebounds, the most in school history.

LSU went years without another deep tournament run. The arrival of Maryland transfer Angel Reese in 2022 proved to be exactly what the Tigers needed. The star forward dominated in the paint. She played especially well during the 2023 NCAA Tournament, averaging 21.3 points and 15.2 rebounds per game. In their first trip to the Final Four in 15 years, the Tigers beat Virginia Tech 79–72 to finally make the national title game. There, LSU finished the job with a 102–85 win over Iowa.

LSU forward Angel Reese earned the SEC Player of the Year Award as a senior in 2023–24.

## BIG-TIME HIRE

Kim Mulkey is known for her intensity—and for winning. The fiery head coach led Baylor to national titles in 2005, 2012, and 2019. In 2021, LSU hired her to do the same with the Tigers. Mulkey's first NCAA Tournament at LSU ended in a second-round upset loss. But with Angel Reese leading the way, the Tigers finally won it all in 2023. The victory made Mulkey the first women's coach to win national titles with two teams.

## FACT BOX

**First Season:** 1975–76

**Location:** Baton Rouge, Louisiana

**Arena:** Pete Maravich Assembly Center

**Conference:** Southeastern Conference

**All-Time Record:** 1,073–507

**NCAA Tournament Appearances:** 30

**Final Fours:** 6

**National Titles:** 2023

**Top Coaches:** Sue Gunter (1982–2004); Kim Mulkey (2021– )

**Top Players:** Julie Gross (1976–80); Joyce Walker (1980–84); Pokey Chatman (1987–91); Cornelia Gayden (1991–95); Temeka Johnson (2001–05); Seimone Augustus (2002–06); Sylvia Fowles (2004–08); Angel Reese (2022–24)

**Mascot:** Mike the Tiger

Angel Reese finished with 15 points and ten rebounds for her 34th double-double of the season, setting an NCAA record.

# MUST-SEE TV

Fans were drawn to smooth-shooting Iowa guard Caitlin Clark throughout the 2022–23 season. But LSU had its own superstar in physical forward Angel Reese. Their meeting in the 2023 NCAA title game was one of the sport's most anticipated games ever.

The final score wasn't close. LSU won 102–85. With an average TV audience of 9.9 million viewers, at the time it was the most-watched women's college basketball game.

Caitlin Clark buried eight three-pointers and scored with a game-high 30 points.

# LOUISIANA TECH LADY TECHSTERS

Guard Kim Mulkey, *right*, won her first 54 games while playing for the Lady Techsters. Old Dominion ended the winning streak in January 1982.

Sonja Hogg graduated from Louisiana Tech in 1968. In 1974, she created the women's basketball team. A fellow alum, Leon Barmore, helped her get the team started while he coached at a local high school.

Hogg led the Lady Techsters to immediate success. After four straight

## WHAT A RUN

The Lady Techsters reached the Final Four in each of Kim Mulkey's seasons there. Two of those teams won national titles. And her winning didn't stop there. Mulkey helped Team USA win an Olympic gold medal in 1984. Later, as a coach, she led Baylor and LSU to national titles.

winning seasons, Louisiana Tech reached its first AIAW Tournament in 1979. The team then got all the way to the title game before falling to Old Dominion 75–65. The Lady Techsters were back in the Final Four the next year. Once again they fell to Old Dominion.

A freshman point guard named Kim Mulkey arrived in 1980–81. The Louisiana native partnered with All-America forward Pam Kelly to lead the Lady Techsters into the AIAW Tournament undefeated. They stayed perfect, ultimately beating Tennessee 79–59 to win their first national title. The team won another title in 1982, though this time in the first NCAA Tournament. The Lady Techsters beat Cheyney 76–62 in the final.

Lady Techsters guard Teresa Weatherspoon celebrates after winning the 1988 NCAA championship.

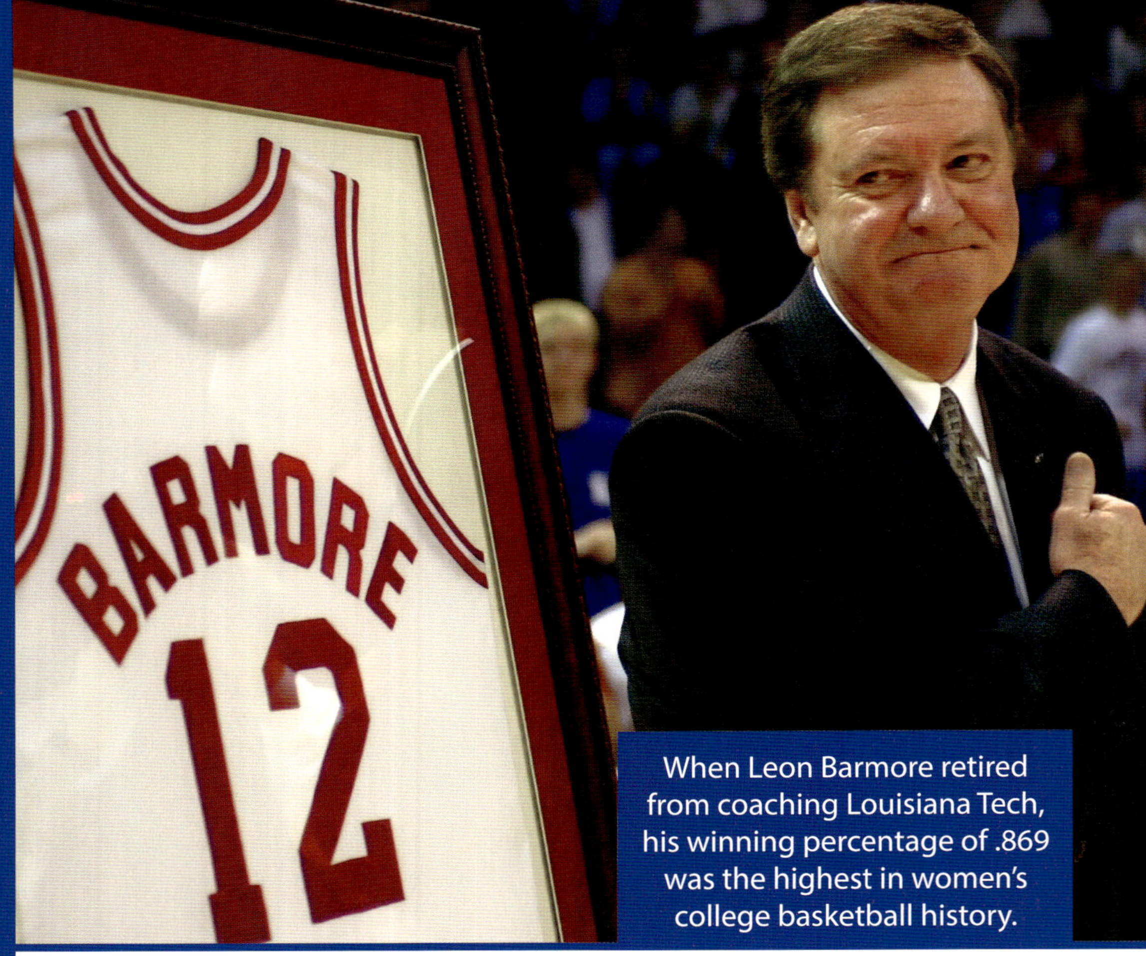


When Leon Barmore retired from coaching Louisiana Tech, his winning percentage of .869 was the highest in women's college basketball history.

Barmore had been an assistant coach at Louisiana Tech since 1977. Prior to the 1982–83 season, he became co–head coach alongside Hogg. The duo led the Techsters back to the national championship game that year. But USC beat the Lady Techsters 69–67. USC then beat the Lady Techsters again in the 1984 Final Four.

Mulkey left after that, but the team found a talented replacement in Teresa Weatherspoon. The tenacious point guard racked up steals and assists. After the Lady Techsters fell in the Elite Eight in 1985 and 1986, Weatherspoon led them back to the Final Four in 1987. A year later, the Lady Techsters returned to the championship game. This time, Weatherspoon's defense lifted Tech to a 56–54 win over Auburn.

Barmore had taken over as the team's sole head coach in 1985. He remained in that role until 2002. Over his 20 total seasons, the Lady Techsters reached nine Final Fours. Replacing him has proven difficult, however. Weatherspoon came back to coach for five seasons, leading the team to NCAA Tournament berths in 2010 and 2011. After that, the Lady Techsters went more than a decade without qualifying again.

## FACT BOX

**First Season:** 1974–75

**Location:** Ruston, Louisiana

**Arena:** Thomas Assembly Center

**Conference:** Conference USA

**All-Time Record:** 1,225–422

**NCAA Tournament Appearances:** 27

**Final Fours:** 10

**National Titles:** 1981,* 1982, 1988

**Top Coaches:** Sonja Hogg (1974–85); Leon Barmore (1982–2002)

**Top Players:** Pam Kelly (1978–82); Kim Mulkey (1980–84); Janice Lawrence (1980–84); Pam Gant (1981–85); Teresa Weatherspoon (1984–88); Venus Lacy (1987–90); Vickie Johnson (1992–96); Adrienne Johnson (2007–11)

**Mascot:** Champ

*AIAW

# LOUISVILLE CARDINALS

The women's basketball program at Louisville dates to 1975, when the AIAW ran the sport. The Cardinals first reached the NCAA Tournament in 1983. They got back ten more times through 2007. However, Louisville never advanced past the second round.

The hiring of coach Jeff Walz in 2007 provided a major boost to the program. Behind junior forward Angel McCoughtry, Louisville reached the 2008 NCAA Tournament. She scored 24 points in the second round to help the Cardinals beat Kansas State and reach their first Sweet 16.

Louisville forward Angel McCoughtry averaged a career-high 23.8 points per game as a junior in 2007–08.

## ANGEL ON FIRE

Angel McCoughtry led the Big East Conference in scoring, rebounds, and steals as a sophomore in 2006–07. That kick-started a prolific career. Her scoring and defensive prowess led the Cardinals to the 2009 NCAA title game. She later went on to a decorated pro career and won two Olympic gold medals with Team USA.

McCoughtry led Louisville on a deeper run in 2009. That year, she helped the No. 3 seed Cardinals upset No. 2 seed Baylor in the Sweet 16. Then they beat No. 1 seed Maryland in the Elite Eight. Playing in their first Final Four, the Cardinals took down No. 1 seed Oklahoma 61–59. However, the dream run ended in the championship game. UConn beat Louisville 76–54.

The Cardinals entered the 2013 NCAA Tournament as

Louisville guard Asia Durr won ACC Player of the Year honors in 2017–18 and 2018–19.

a No. 5 seed. They matched up with No. 1 seed Baylor, the defending champion, in the Sweet 16. With 2.6 seconds left, Louisville's Monique Reid went to the free-throw line with her team trailing 81–80. The senior forward calmly knocked them both down to secure a shocking upset. The Cardinals kept rolling from there. Upsets over Tennessee and California sent Louisville back to the title game. However, the Cardinals once again fell to UConn.

Louisville guard Hailey Van Lith celebrates the Cardinals making the Final Four in 2022.

The 2017–18 Cardinals were stacked. All-Americans Asia Durr and Myisha Hines-Allen led a team that featured six future WNBA players. For the first time, Louisville entered the NCAA Tournament as a No. 1 seed. The team then got all the way to the Final Four before falling to Mississippi State.

The Cardinals remained competitive. In 2019 and 2021, they reached the Elite Eight. In 2022, sophomore guard Hailey Van Lith carried the Cardinals back to the Final Four.

## FACT BOX

**First Season:** 1975–76

**Location:** Louisville, Kentucky

**Arena:** KFC Yum! Center

**Conference:** Atlantic Coast Conference

**All-Time Record:** 1,033–537

**NCAA Tournament Appearances:** 27

**Final Fours:** 4

**National Titles:** None

**Top Coaches:** Jeff Walz (2007– )

**Top Players:** Angel McCoughtry (2005–09); Shoni Schimmel (2010–14); Myisha Hines-Allen (2014–18); Asia Durr (2015–19); Dana Evans (2017–21); Hailey Van Lith (2020–23)

**Mascot:** Louie the Cardinal

# MARYLAND TERRAPINS

Maryland proved to be a competitive team from its start in 1971–72. The Terrapins reached their first AIAW Tournament in 1974. In 1978, they got all the way to the championship game. And four years later, in 1982, they reached the first NCAA Tournament. A standout performance by junior guard Jasmina Perazic helped Maryland get all the way to the Final Four. However, Cheyney ended the Terrapins' run there.

Maryland forward Crystal Langhorne won the ACC Player of the Year Award as a senior in 2007–08.

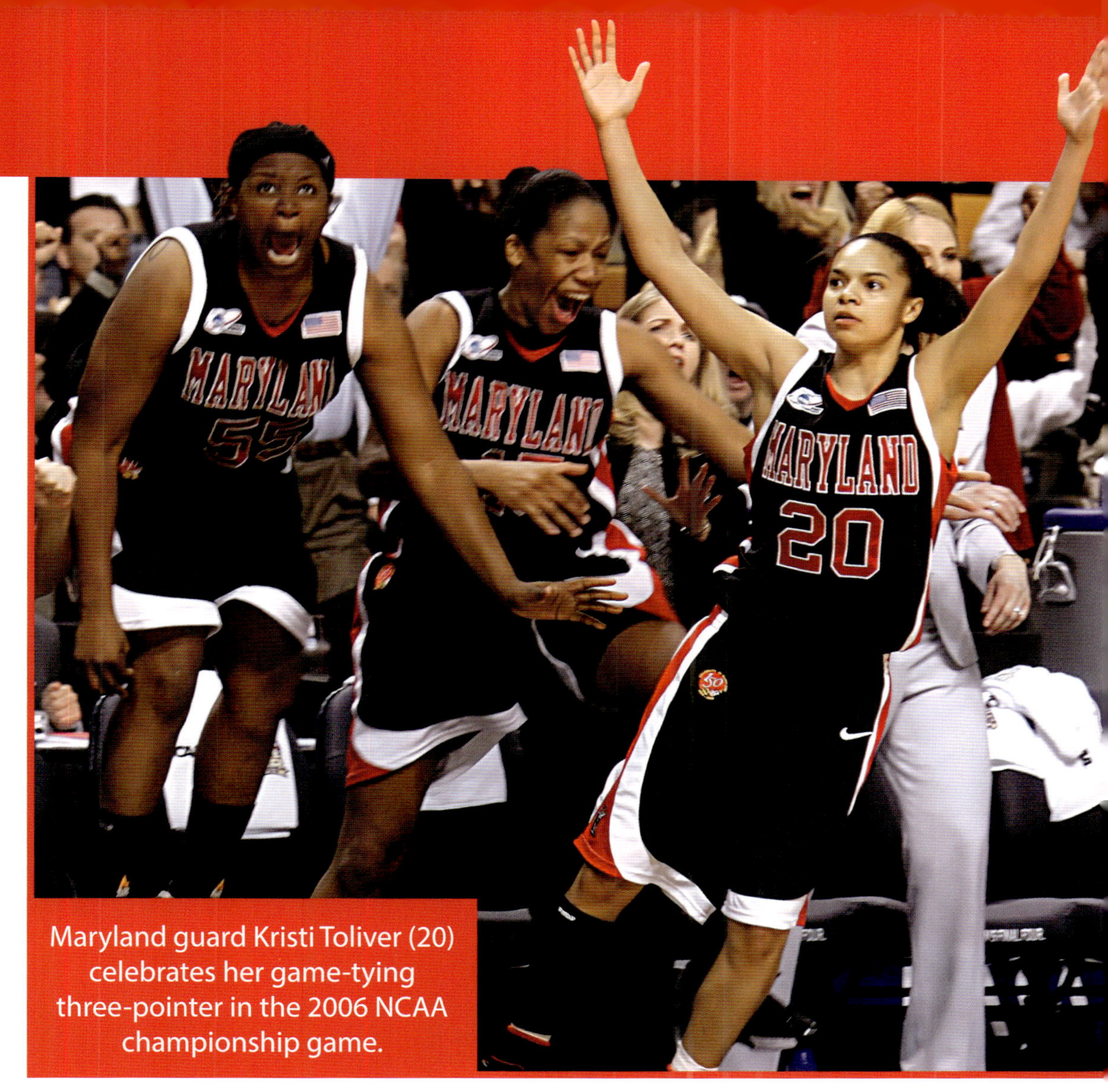


Maryland guard Kristi Toliver (20) celebrates her game-tying three-pointer in the 2006 NCAA championship game.

Much of the team's early success came under Chris Weller. She coached the team from 1975–76 until 2001–02. The Terrapins made ten of the first 12 NCAA Tournaments, from 1982 to 1993. Their best run came in 1989, when All-America forward Vicky Bullett guided Maryland back to the Final Four. However, the Terrapins eventually fell off. They made the tournament just twice from 1994 to 2002.

## THOMAS LEADS THE WAY

Senior forward Alyssa Thomas caught fire for Maryland in the 2014 NCAA Tournament. The three-time ACC Player of the Year posted four straight double-doubles to send the No. 4 seed Terrapins back to the Final Four. However, Notre Dame ended their season there.

The team rebounded soon after Brenda Frese became coach in 2002–03. All-America sophomore forward Crystal Langhorne led a loaded team in 2005–06. In the Final Four, Maryland beat conference foe North Carolina to reach its first championship game. Duke, another conference rival, awaited the Terrapins.

Duke had beaten Maryland twice in the regular season. Another Maryland loss looked likely when Duke

Maryland forward Alyssa Thomas led the ACC in points, rebounds, and assists per game as a junior in 2012–13.

took a 13-point lead in the first half. But the Terrapins clawed their way back.

With less than 10 seconds to play, Maryland had narrowed Duke's lead to three. Then freshman guard Kristi Toliver erased the lead by draining a three-pointer to send the game to overtime. Toliver then hit a go-ahead free throw in overtime to help the Terrapins win their first national title.

## FACT BOX

**First Season:** 1971–72

**Location:** College Park, Maryland

**Arena:** Xfinity Center

**Conference:** Big Ten Conference

**All-Time Record:** 1,150–472

**NCAA Tournament Appearances:** 32

**Final Fours:** 5

**National Titles:** 2006

**Top Coaches:** Chris Weller (1975–2002); Brenda Frese (2002– )

**Top Players:** Jasmina Perazic (1979–83); Vicky Bullett (1985–89); Crystal Langhorne (2004–08); Kristi Toliver (2005–09); Marissa Coleman (2005–09); Alyssa Thomas (2010–14); Lexie Brown (2013–15); Brionna Jones (2013–17); Shatori Walker-Kimbrough (2013–17)

**Mascot:** Testudo

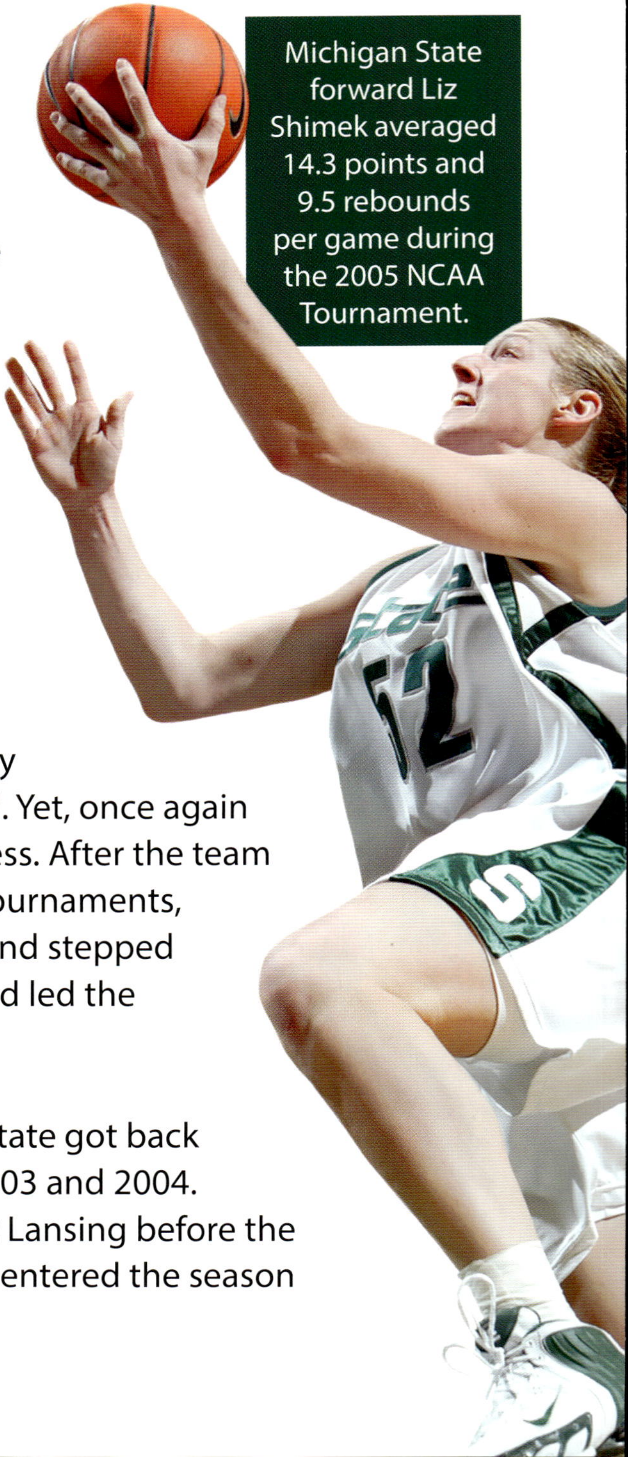

Michigan State forward Liz Shimek averaged 14.3 points and 9.5 rebounds per game during the 2005 NCAA Tournament.

Michigan State created its women's basketball program in 1972–73. The team struggled for many of its early seasons. One bright spot came in 1990–91. The Spartans won 21 games. That marked their best record since 1977–78 and sent them to their first NCAA Tournament. However, consistent success remained out of reach.

The Spartans reached the NCAA Tournament again in 1996 and 1997. Both times they advanced to the second round. Yet, once again they couldn't sustain the success. After the team missed the next three NCAA Tournaments, longtime coach Karen Langeland stepped down. Over 24 seasons, she had led the team to a record of 376–290.

Under new coach Joanne Palombo-McCallie, Michigan State got back to the NCAA Tournament in 2003 and 2004. Expectations were high in East Lansing before the 2004–05 season. The Spartans entered the season

Forward Aerial Powers earned All–Big Ten honors all three seasons she played at Michigan State from 2013 to 2016.

ranked No. 15 in the nation. That marked the first time they had earned a preseason ranking. The team then lived up to those expectations by finishing tied for first in the Big Ten and winning the conference tournament for the first time.

The Spartans entered the NCAA Tournament as a No. 1 seed and riding a 12-game winning streak. They avoided an upset against No. 8 seed USC in the second round when Rene Haynes scored the game-winning layup in the final seconds. Liz Shimek took over after that. The junior forward recorded a double-double in an Elite Eight win over Stanford. Then she did

## READY TO DANCE

The Spartans finally broke through and made their first NCAA Tournament in 1991. Senior guard Eileen Shea was ready for the big stage. She dropped 35 points in the team's opener against Oklahoma State, a mark that remained a school record for an NCAA Tournament game through 2025. Her scoring wasn't enough, though, as Oklahoma State won 96–94.

Spartans guard Tori Jankoska led the Big Ten in scoring with 22.6 points per game as a senior in 2016–17.

it again against Tennessee in the Final Four to help send the Spartans to their first national championship game. The dream run ended there, however, as the Spartans fell 84–62 to Baylor.

Michigan State remained a consistent NCAA Tournament qualifier after that. However, after making the Sweet 16 in 2006, the Spartans did so just once more through 2025. Several great players shined for the Spartans during that time. High-scoring forward Aerial Powers earned All-America honors in 2015–16. In 2017, guard Tori Jankoska finished her four-year career with 2,212 points, the most in school history.

## FACT BOX

**First Season:** 1972–73

**Location:** East Lansing, Michigan

**Arena:** Breslin Student Events Center

**Conference:** Big Ten Conference

**All-Time Record:** 934–598

**NCAA Tournament Appearances:** 20

**Final Fours:** 1

**National Titles:** None

**Top Coaches:** Karen Langeland (1976–2000); Joanne Palombo-McCallie (2000–07)

**Top Players:** Kristin Haynie (2001–05); Lindsay Bowen (2002–06); Liz Shimek (2002–06); Allyssa DeHaan (2006–10); Kalisha Keane (2007–11); Aerial Powers (2013–16); Tori Jankoska (2013–17); Nia Clouden (2018–22)

**Mascot:** Sparty

# MISSISSIPPI STATE BULLDOGS

Winning seasons were rare in Mississippi State's early seasons. Founded in 1974–75, the program went through five coaches in its first 20 seasons. All five left with losing records.

Before the 1995–96 season, the school hired Sharon Fanning-Otis to be the Bulldogs' sixth coach. Early on, it looked as if she would suffer a fate similar to the others. Her first three teams posted losing records. By her fourth season, though, Fanning-Otis led the Bulldogs to a 17–11 record and the 1999 NCAA Tournament.

The Bulldogs remained a mostly winning team after that. Fanning-Otis led them to a sixth NCAA Tournament in 2010. She coached two more seasons before retiring in 2012 with a school-best record of 281–232.

Mississippi State didn't reach another NCAA Tournament

Mississippi State reached its first Sweet 16 in 2010. Alexis Rack scored 30 points in an 87–67 second-round upset over No. 2 seed Ohio State.

Mississippi State guard Morgan William (2) releases her game-winning shot against UConn in the 2017 Final Four.

until 2015, under third-year coach Vic Schaefer. After losing in the second round that year, the Bulldogs got to the Sweet 16 in 2016. However, they were destroyed by UConn, losing 98–38.

Mississippi State responded with its best season yet in 2016–17. Behind 41 points from junior guard Morgan William, the Bulldogs took down Baylor 94–85 in overtime in the Elite Eight. That set up a rematch with UConn in the Final Four. William stepped up in overtime. As time expired, the 5-foot-5-inch star pulled up for a game-winning jumper.

## ANOTHER RUN

Victoria Vivians and Teaira McCowan led Mississippi State's 2017–18 team. Behind the All-America duo, the Bulldogs reeled off a 32-game winning streak to start the season. McCowan later set a Final Four record when she grabbed 25 rebounds in a 73–63 overtime win over Louisville in the national semifinal.

Bulldogs center Teaira McCowan won the SEC Player of the Year Award in 2018–19.

William's shot fell perfectly through the hoop. The basket not only secured a Bulldogs win but also snapped UConn's NCAA-record 111-game winning streak. The play left many people in college basketball stunned. It's still considered one of the biggest upsets in college basketball history.

Mississippi State fell short of a fairy-tale finish, losing to

SEC rival South Carolina in the championship game. But the Bulldogs had emerged as a national power. In 2018, the team reached a second consecutive title game. The Bulldogs were seconds away from a championship but fell to Notre Dame on a buzzer-beater.

The Bulldogs came back to reach the Elite Eight in 2019. Then they were 27–6 when the 2019–20 season was canceled due to COVID-19. Schaefer left for a new job after that. Sam Purcell took over in 2022–23 and led the Bulldogs to the NCAA Tournament twice in his first three seasons.

## FACT BOX

**First Season:** 1974–75

**Location:** Starkville, Mississippi

**Arena:** Humphrey Coliseum

**Conference:** Southeastern Conference

**All-Time Record:** 842–679

**NCAA Tournament Appearances:** 13

**Final Fours:** 2

**National Titles:** None

**Top Coaches:** Sharon Fanning-Otis (1995–2012); Vic Schaefer (2012–20)

**Top Players:** LaToya Thomas (1999–2003); Tan White (2001–05); Alexis Rack (2006–10); Victoria Vivians (2014–18); Morgan William (2014–18); Teaira McCowan (2015–19)

**Mascot:** Bully

# MISSOURI STATE BEARS

The women's basketball team at Southwest Missouri State began in 1969–70 as a Division II program. After 13 seasons, the school today known as Missouri State jumped up to Division I for the 1982–83 season. By the end of the decade, the Bears were emerging as a strong program.

Cheryl Burnett coached Missouri State to ten NCAA Tournaments, including the Final Four in 1992 and 2001.

Cheryl Burnett was a big reason for that success. She became the Bears' coach in 1987–88. By 1989–90, the team tied for the best record in its conference. A year later, the Bears won their conference tournament to make their first NCAA Tournament.

The No. 8 seed Bears easily beat Tennessee Tech 94–64 in the opener. Then they played well against eventual champion Tennessee in the second round before losing 55–47. Legendary Lady Volunteers coach Pat Summitt said it was the toughest defense her team had seen all season.

## SENSATIONAL SCORER

Few in college basketball history could score like Jackie Stiles. The standout guard finished her career in 2001 with 3,393 points, the most in women's NCAA basketball history at the time. As a junior, she piled up 56 points in a win against Evansville. At that time, only three players had scored more in a game. The following year, she became the first woman to score more than 1,000 points in an NCAA season.

The Bears kept it up in 1991–92. Behind their tenacious, full-court defensive pressure, they won 21 consecutive games. Returning to the NCAA Tournament as a No. 8 seed, Missouri State put together an even deeper run.

The Bears opened with a 75–59 win over Kansas. Next up was No. 1 seed Iowa on the Hawkeyes' home court. Bears sophomore guard Melody Howard drained a three-pointer in the final minute to send

Guard Jackie Stiles averaged more than 20 points per game all four years she played at Missouri State from 1997 to 2001.

Missouri State guard Brice Calip (11) goes up for a shot during an NCAA Tournament game in 2019.

the game to overtime. Then junior forward Secelia Winkfield buried a shot with 1.5 seconds left to secure a shocking 61–60 win.

The Bears then cruised to blowout wins over UCLA and Ole Miss. That made them the first No. 8 seed to make the Final Four. The unlikely run ended there, however, as Missouri State fell 84–72 to Western Kentucky.

From 1991 to 2006, the Bears missed the NCAA Tournament only three times. The highlight came in 2001. Behind three-time Missouri Valley Conference (MVC) Player of the Year Jackie Stiles, the No. 5 seed Bears made another run to the Final Four. The team's quest to reach its first NCAA title game ended with an 81–64 loss to No. 3 seed Purdue.

Burnett left after the 2001–02 season. Missouri State remained competitive in the MVC. However, the Bears reached the NCAA Tournament only four times between 2007 and 2025.

## FACT BOX

**First Season:** 1969–70

**Location:** Springfield, Missouri

**Arena:** Great Southern Bank Arena

**Conference:** Missouri Valley Conference

**All-Time Record:** 1,019–648

**NCAA Tournament Appearances:** 17

**Final Fours:** 2

**National Titles:** None

**Top Coaches:** Cheryl Burnett (1987–2002)

**Top Players:** Secelia Winkfield (1989–93); Melody Howard (1990–94); Tina Robbins (1990–94); Jackie Stiles (1997–2001); Kari Koch (2002–06); Casey Garrison (2008–12); Tyonna Snow (2012–16); Brice Calip (2016–22)

**Mascot:** Boomer the Bear

# NORTH CAROLINA TAR HEELS

North Carolina finished its first season in 1974–75 with a 15–3 record. However, that wasn't enough for the team to qualify for the AIAW Tournament. The Tar Heels finally qualified for their first major postseason tournament in 1983. By then they were playing in the NCAA.

That season the Tar Heels began a five-year streak of reaching the NCAA Tournament. Their best showings came in 1984 and 1986. Two-time ACC Player of the Year Pam Leake helped the team reach the Sweet 16 both seasons.

The Tar Heels made the 1987 tournament under first-year coach Sylvia Hatchell. That was followed by four losing seasons.

North Carolina plays its home games at Carmichael Arena.

North Carolina players celebrate winning the 1994 NCAA championship.

North Carolina stuck with the coach, though, and that soon paid off.

Charlotte Smith joined the team in 1991–92. The forward from Shelby, North Carolina, proved to be a strong scorer and rebounder as she led the Tar Heels back to the NCAA Tournament. By her junior year, North Carolina was one of the best teams in the country. As a No. 3 seed, North Carolina upset No. 2 Vanderbilt and No. 1 UConn on the way to the Final Four. There, Smith poured in 23 points to take down another No. 1 seed in Purdue.

North Carolina faced No. 4 seed Louisiana Tech in the title game. With 0.7 seconds left, the Lady Techsters led 59–57. Smith then hit a three-pointer to win it. North Carolina became the first No. 3 seed to win a national title.

The Tar Heels remained a strong team under Hatchell. They missed the NCAA Tournament only three times between 1992 and 2015.

Guard Ivory Latta earned All-America honors three times at North Carolina from 2003 to 2007.

## BIG-TIME SCORER

Ivory Latta starred in North Carolina's runs to the 2006 and 2007 Final Fours. The sharpshooting guard from South Carolina eventually set several team records, including for points (2,285), three-pointers (345), and free-throw percentage (.840). The US Basketball Writers Association named her its 2005–06 National Player of the Year.

Behind star guard Ivory Latta, they reached back-to-back Final Fours in 2006 and 2007. By 2019, Hatchell had become only the third women's basketball coach to win 1,000 games. However, players said she had used racially insensitive language and made some of them play through injuries. Hatchell resigned after 33 seasons with North Carolina.

Under new coach Courtney Banghart, the Tar Heels soon began a new era of success. North Carolina reached its fifth straight NCAA Tournament in 2025. Two of those runs ended in the Sweet 16.

## FACT BOX

**First Season:** 1974–75

**Location:** Chapel Hill, North Carolina

**Arena:** Carmichael Arena

**Conference:** Atlantic Coast Conference

**All-Time Record:** 1,094–519

**NCAA Tournament Appearances:** 32

**Final Fours:** 3

**National Titles:** 1994

**Top Coaches:** Sylvia Hatchell (1986–2019)

**Top Players:** Tresa Brown (1981–84); Pam Leake (1982–86); Tonya Sampson (1990–94); Charlotte Smith (1991–95); Marion Jones (1993–95, 1996–97); Tracy Reid (1994–98); Ivory Latta (2003–07); Erlana Larkins (2004–08)

**Mascot:** Rameses

# NORTH CAROLINA STATE WOLFPACK

After just one season, North Carolina State needed a new coach. The team hired Kay Yow for that role in 1975. She ended up staying in the position for more than three decades until 2009. During that time, she racked up nearly 700 wins while also inspiring fans with her courageous battle with breast cancer.

The team, known as NC State, enjoyed early success under Yow. The 1977–78 squad went undefeated in ACC play. Two years later, the Wolfpack did it again while also winning the conference tournament. That earned the team its first berth into the AIAW Tournament. It also started a run of eight straight seasons making either the AIAW or NCAA tournament.

By 1997–98, Yow had led NC State to 12 NCAA Tournaments. But the Wolfpack never advanced past the Sweet 16. Behind the

NC State coach Kay Yow was voted into the Basketball Hall of Fame in 2002.

## SUCCESSFUL SISTERS

Kay Yow began her head coaching career at Elon College, a small school in North Carolina. There, she coached her younger sister, Susan. When Kay left for NC State in 1975–76, Susan went with her. Susan led the Wolfpack in scoring and rebounding that season while becoming the program's first All-American.

towering duo of 6-foot-3-inch forward Chasity Melvin and 6-foot-6-inch center Summer Erb, the Wolfpack made it to that stage in 1998. There, they upset No. 1 seed Old Dominion 55–54. Then the Wolfpack took down No. 2 seed UConn to reach their first Final Four. Louisiana Tech ended their season there.

Yow's final NCAA Tournament appearance came in 2007. NC State made a run to the Sweet 16 before losing to UConn.

Center Elissa Cunane made 54 percent of her shots at NC State from 2018 to 2022.

By then, Yow had long been battling breast cancer. She had been diagnosed in 1987. Yow remained on the sideline while undergoing treatment in 2007–08. In January 2009, she died at age 66.

Wes Moore took over as NC State's coach in 2013–14. The Wolfpack soon became one of the top teams in the ACC. Behind three-time All-America center Elissa Cunane, the

NC State guard Aziaha James averaged 16.8 points per game in 2023–24.

Wolfpack won three straight ACC Tournament titles starting in 2020. In 2021 and 2022, the team entered the NCAA Tournament as a No. 1 seed. However, neither squad got past the Elite Eight. The Wolfpack tried again as a No. 3 seed in 2024. This time Aziaha James caught fire. The junior guard averaged 23.4 points in the tournament to send NC State on another run to the Final Four.

## FACT BOX

**First Season:** 1974–75

**Location:** Raleigh, North Carolina

**Arena:** James T. Valvano Arena at William Neal Reynolds Coliseum

**Conference:** Atlantic Coast Conference

**All-Time Record:** 1,077–504

**NCAA Tournament Appearances:** 30

**Final Fours:** 2

**National Titles:** None

**Top Coaches:** Kay Yow (1975–2009); Wes Moore (2013– )

**Top Players:** Susan Yow (1975–76); Genia Beasley (1976–80); Trudi Lacey (1977–81); Linda Page (1981–85); Trena Trice (1983–87); Andrea Stinson (1988–91); Chasity Melvin (1994–98); Elissa Cunane (2018–22)

**Mascot:** Mr. and Ms. Wuf

# NOTRE DAME FIGHTING IRISH

Notre Dame enjoyed a lot of wins in the years after its 1977–78 debut. Yet for more than two decades, the Fighting Irish never qualified for a major postseason tournament. Muffet McGraw finally changed that. She took over as the team's coach in 1987–88. In 1992, the Fighting Irish finally qualified for the NCAA Tournament. And more success was on the way.

Notre Dame center Ruth Riley recorded 28 points, 13 rebounds, and seven blocks in the 2001 NCAA championship game.

By the mid-1990s, making the NCAA Tournament was the expectation in South Bend, Indiana. In 1997, Notre Dame became the first No. 6 seed to make the Final Four. Four years later, in 2001, the Irish entered the Big Dance, as the NCAA Tournament came to be known, as a No. 1 seed.

Behind senior center Ruth Riley, that year's Naismith Award winner, the Irish charged to the national title game against Purdue. The Indiana teams were tied 66–66 late when Purdue fouled Riley. With 5.8 seconds left, she buried both free throws to secure the championship.

Notre Dame didn't return to the Final Four for the remainder of the 2000s. In the 2010s, though, the Irish made a habit of going on deep runs in the tournament. Three-time All-America guard Skylar Diggins played a big role. Starting in 2011, she led Notre Dame to three straight Final Fours. In 2011 and 2012, the Fighting Irish played for a national title. However, they fell short each time.

In 2013–14, sophomore Jewell Loyd was one of the best scorers in the country. The All-America guard helped Notre Dame get back to the national championship game in 2014 and again in 2015. But both years, the Irish lost to UConn.

Notre Dame guard Skylar Diggins led the Big East in assists and steals per game as a senior in 2012–13.

## NOTRE DAME LIFER

As a senior in 2000–01, guard Niele Ivey earned All-America honors while helping the Fighting Irish win their first national title. Ivey became an assistant coach at Notre Dame in 2007. When Muffet McGraw retired after the 2019–20 season, Notre Dame hired Ivey as its new head coach.

Notre Dame guard Arike Ogunbowale (24) releases the game-winning shot in the 2018 NCAA championship game.

In 2018, junior guard Arike Ogunbowale guided Notre Dame back to the Final Four. The Irish faced UConn again in the semifinals. Ogunbowale buried a jumper with one second left in overtime to send Notre Dame to the championship game. There, Ogunbowale hit a buzzer-beater against Mississippi State to finally secure Notre Dame's second national title.

Ogunbowale nearly led the Irish to another championship the next year. However, Notre Dame fell just shy in an 82–81 loss to Baylor in the title game. After 33 seasons in charge, McGraw retired in 2020. In 2025, the Irish made their fourth straight Sweet 16 under coach Niele Ivey.

## FACT BOX

**First Season:** 1977–78

**Location:** South Bend, Indiana

**Arena:** Purcell Pavilion

**Conference:** Atlantic Coast Conference

**All-Time Record:** 1,129–389

**NCAA Tournament Appearances:** 30

**Final Fours:** 9

**National Titles:** 2001, 2018

**Top Coaches:** Muffet McGraw (1987–2020); Niele Ivey (2020– )

**Top Players:** Katryna Gaither (1993–97); Ruth Riley (1997–2001); Skylar Diggins (2009–13); Kayla McBride (2010–14); Jewell Loyd (2012–15); Brianna Turner (2014–19); Arike Ogunbowale (2015–19); Hannah Hidalgo (2023– )

**Mascot:** The Leprechaun

# OHIO STATE BUCKEYES

Basketball spread to Columbus, Ohio, soon after it was invented. An Ohio State women's team was playing games as early as 1899. By 1907, however, the program shut down. Nearly six decades later, in 1965, the school created its varsity program.

From early on, the Buckeyes were a winning team. They carried those winning ways into the sport's NCAA era beginning in 1981–82, missing the tournament just one time during the decade. However, the Buckeyes didn't go on their first deep postseason run until 1993. Led by star freshman guard Katie Smith, the team earned a No. 1 seed. Then it won three games to reach the Final Four. Facing Big Ten rival Iowa, Smith hit a shot with five seconds left to send the game to overtime. Forward Nikki Keyton's clutch free throws with 33 seconds left sealed the 73–72 win.

That set up a meeting with No. 2 seed Texas Tech in the national title game.

Ohio State center Jessica Davenport (50) led the Big Ten in points, rebounds, and blocks per game in 2006–07.

Starting in 2008–09, Ohio State center Jantel Lavender (42) led the Big Ten in scoring for three straight years.

This one was almost as close. Despite 28 points from Smith, the Buckeyes fell 84–82.

Ohio State reached the NCAA Tournament only two times in the next nine seasons. Jessica Davenport helped turn things around. The sophomore center won her first of three Big Ten Player of the Year Awards in 2004–05. She also lifted the Buckeyes to three straight regular-season Big Ten titles.

Jantel Lavender picked up where Davenport left off. The center won Big Ten Player of the Year honors all four years at Ohio State. And she led the Buckeyes to three straight Big Ten Tournament titles from 2009 to 2011.

Guard Kelsey Mitchell led the Big Ten in scoring as a freshman in 2014–15. The Cincinnati native averaged at least 22.6 points per game during her four seasons. When she left

From 2016 to 2018, Buckeyes guard Kelsey Mitchell set a college basketball record by making a three-pointer in 92 consecutive games.

## BIG TEN DARLINGS

The Big Ten only began sponsoring women's sports in 1981. Ohio State won the conference's first women's basketball tournament in 1982. Though the Big Ten waited 13 years to hold another one, the Buckeyes took over the regular season. They won or shared the Big Ten title five times in six years starting in 1982–83.

Ohio State, she ranked second in NCAA women's basketball history with 3,402 career points.

Despite having so many great players, Ohio State went decades without another Final Four appearance. In 2023, the Buckeyes upset UConn in the Sweet 16. The result marked UConn's worst finish in 18 years and Ohio State's first trip to the Elite Eight since the 1993 run to the title game. However, the Buckeyes lost to top-seeded Virginia Tech, and the quest for another Final Four continued.

## FACT BOX

**First Season:** 1965–66

**Location:** Columbus, Ohio

**Arena:** Value City Arena at the Jerome Schottenstein Center

**Conference:** Big Ten Conference

**All-Time Record:** 1,127–494

**NCAA Tournament Appearances:** 29

**Final Fours:** 1

**National Titles:** None

**Top Coaches:** Nancy Darsch (1985–97); Jim Foster (2002–13); Kevin McGuff (2013– )

**Top Players:** Frani Washington (1977–80); Tracey Hall (1984–88); Nikita Lowry (1985–89); Katie Smith (1992–96); Jessica Davenport (2003–07); Jantel Lavender (2007–11); Samantha Prahalis (2008–12); Kelsey Mitchell (2014–18)

**Mascot:** Brutus Buckeye

# OKLAHOMA SOONERS

Established in 1974–75, Oklahoma's women's basketball team often struggled in its early years. The Sooners reached the NCAA Tournament only two times in their first 24 seasons. Coach Sherri Coale eventually changed that. Yet even that took time.

Oklahoma guard Stacey Dales averaged 15.3 points per game during the 2002 NCAA Tournament.

Coale took over as coach in 1996–97. The Sooners went 5–22. They barely improved the next season, winning eight games. But by 1999–2000, the pieces were in place. The Sooners began a streak of 19 straight seasons reaching the NCAA Tournament. Several of those years included deep runs.

Behind senior guard Stacey Dales, the two-time Big 12 Player of the Year, Oklahoma got all the way to the 2002 national title game. The Sooners dominated on the way there, winning all five tournament games by at least 10 points. However, the hot streak ended in the final with an 82–70 loss to UConn.

Courtney Paris propelled the next great era of Oklahoma basketball. The powerful 6-foot-4-inch center became the first woman to earn All-America honors four times, from 2005–06 to 2008–09. During that time, she became the first woman to pull down 2,000 rebounds. She also shattered an NCAA record with 112 consecutive double-doubles.

The Sooners' best season with Paris was her last. Teaming up with sophomore guard Danielle Robinson, she led the No. 1–seeded Sooners to the Final Four. Paris recorded 16 points and 16 rebounds against Louisville. However, Oklahoma lost 61–59.

Behind Robinson and senior guard Nyeshia Stevenson, the Sooners stayed strong in 2009–10. Stevenson poured in 31 points in an Elite Eight win over Kentucky. Robinson and Stevenson then scored a combined total of 38 points in the national semifinal. However, the Sooners fell to Stanford 73–66.

Center Courtney Paris averaged 19.9 points and 14.8 rebounds per game during her career at Oklahoma from 2005 to 2009.

The Sooners' NCAA Tournament streak ended in 2019. Coale stepped down two years later. Under new coach Jennie Baranczyk, a new streak began in 2022. Two years later, senior guard Skylar Vann was named co–Big 12 Player of the Year. She helped the Sooners win the Big 12 during their last season in the conference. Oklahoma began playing in the SEC in 2024–25.

Oklahoma guard Danielle Robinson averaged 16 points and 6.2 assists per game during the 2010 NCAA Tournament.

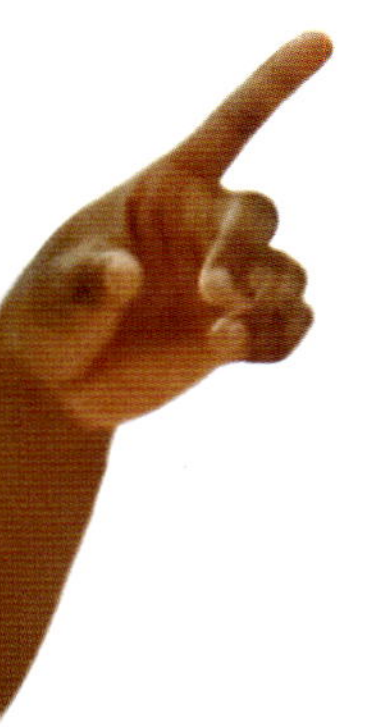

## STAYING ALIVE

Oklahoma reached its first NCAA Tournament in 1986. By 1990, the team was a mess. The Sooners finished just 7–22. Attendance was dismal. So the school announced it was shutting the program down. After public outcry, Oklahoma reversed that decision eight days later.

## FACT BOX

**First Season:** 1974–75

**Location:** Norman, Oklahoma

**Arena:** Lloyd Noble Center

**Conference:** Southeastern Conference

**All-Time Record:** 938–622

**NCAA Tournament Appearances:** 25

**Final Fours:** 3

**National Titles:** None

**Top Coaches:** Sherri Coale (1996–2021)

**Top Players:** Stacey Dales (1997–2002); LaNeishea Caufield (1998–2002); Courtney Paris (2005–09); Danielle Robinson (2007–11); Madi Williams (2018–23); Skylar Vann (2020–25)

**Mascot:** Boomer and Sooner

# OLD DOMINION MONARCHS

Old Dominion played its first game in 1969. Women's college basketball was still in its infancy. Before long, the school from Norfolk, Virginia, was one of the sport's powers.

Point guard Nancy Lieberman and power forward Inge Nissen joined the team in 1976–77. They led the Monarchs to the National Women's Invitational Tournament (NWIT) semifinals as freshmen. Old Dominion won the NWIT the next year. Then the team reached its first AIAW Tournament in 1979. After taking down defending champion UCLA in the semifinals, Old Dominion met Louisiana Tech for the title. The Lady Techsters jumped out to a 32–27 lead. Then Lieberman and Nissen took over. The duo scored a combined total of 42 points in a 75–65 win.

Old Dominion guard Nancy Lieberman was voted into the Basketball Hall of Fame in 1996.

Already a national power, the Monarchs added another weapon for Lieberman and Nissen's senior season in 1979–80. Freshman Anne Donovan, a 6-foot-8-inch center, was dominant. In that year's AIAW title game, she racked up 17 rebounds and ten blocks. Old Dominion easily outlasted Tennessee to win 68–53 and defend its championship.

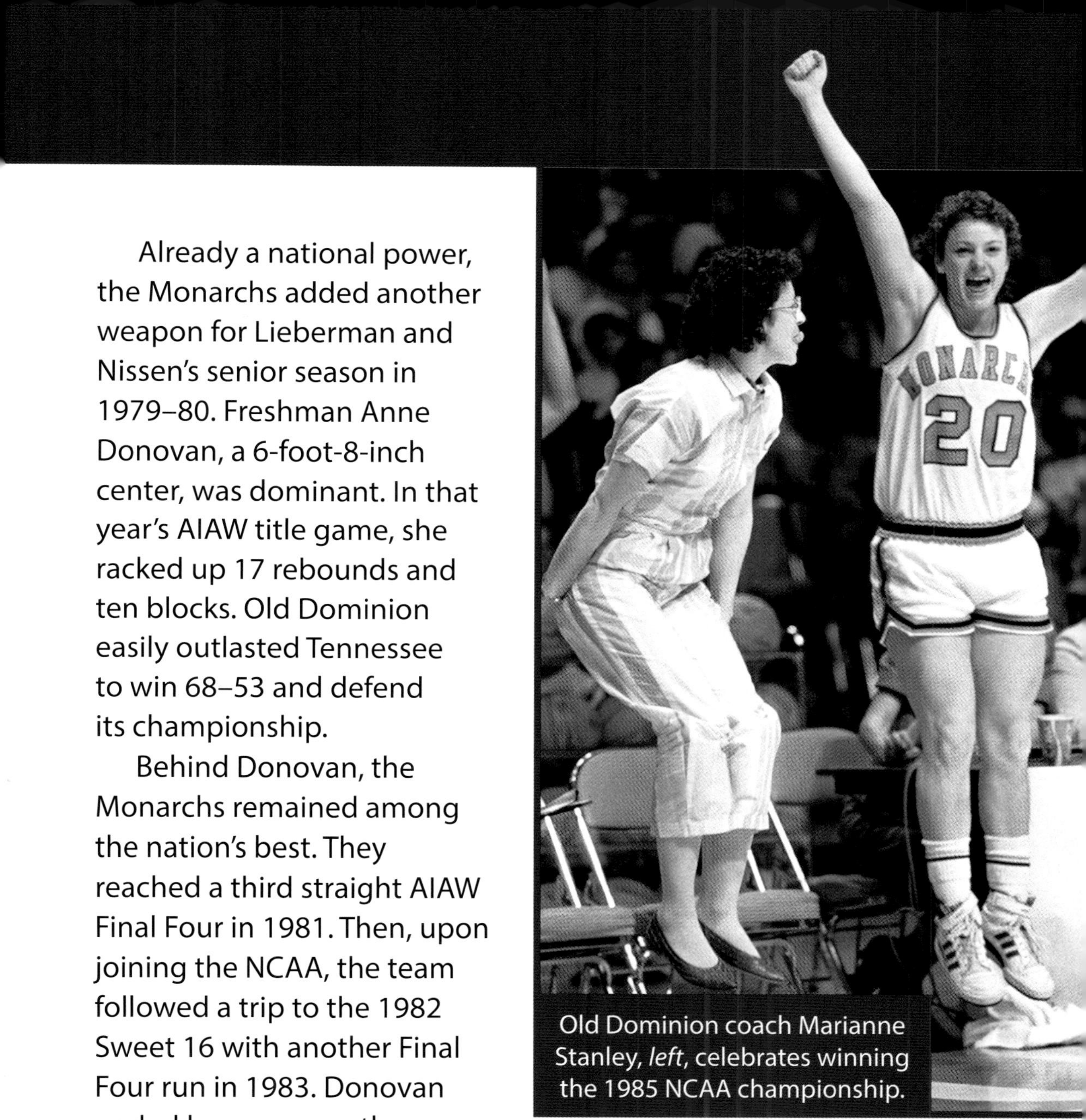

Old Dominion coach Marianne Stanley, *left*, celebrates winning the 1985 NCAA championship.

Behind Donovan, the Monarchs remained among the nation's best. They reached a third straight AIAW Final Four in 1981. Then, upon joining the NCAA, the team followed a trip to the 1982 Sweet 16 with another Final Four run in 1983. Donovan ended her career as the winner of the first women's Naismith Award.

Needing to retool, the Monarchs brought in transfers Medina Dixon and Tracy Claxton. As seniors in 1984–85, the forward duo led Old Dominion on another run to the

## GOING GLOBAL

As women's basketball grew, Old Dominion needed to find creative ways to keep up with bigger schools. One way the Monarchs did so was by finding talented players from overseas. Ticha Penicheiro was one of the best. The point guard from Portugal starred on the 1997 national runner-up team.

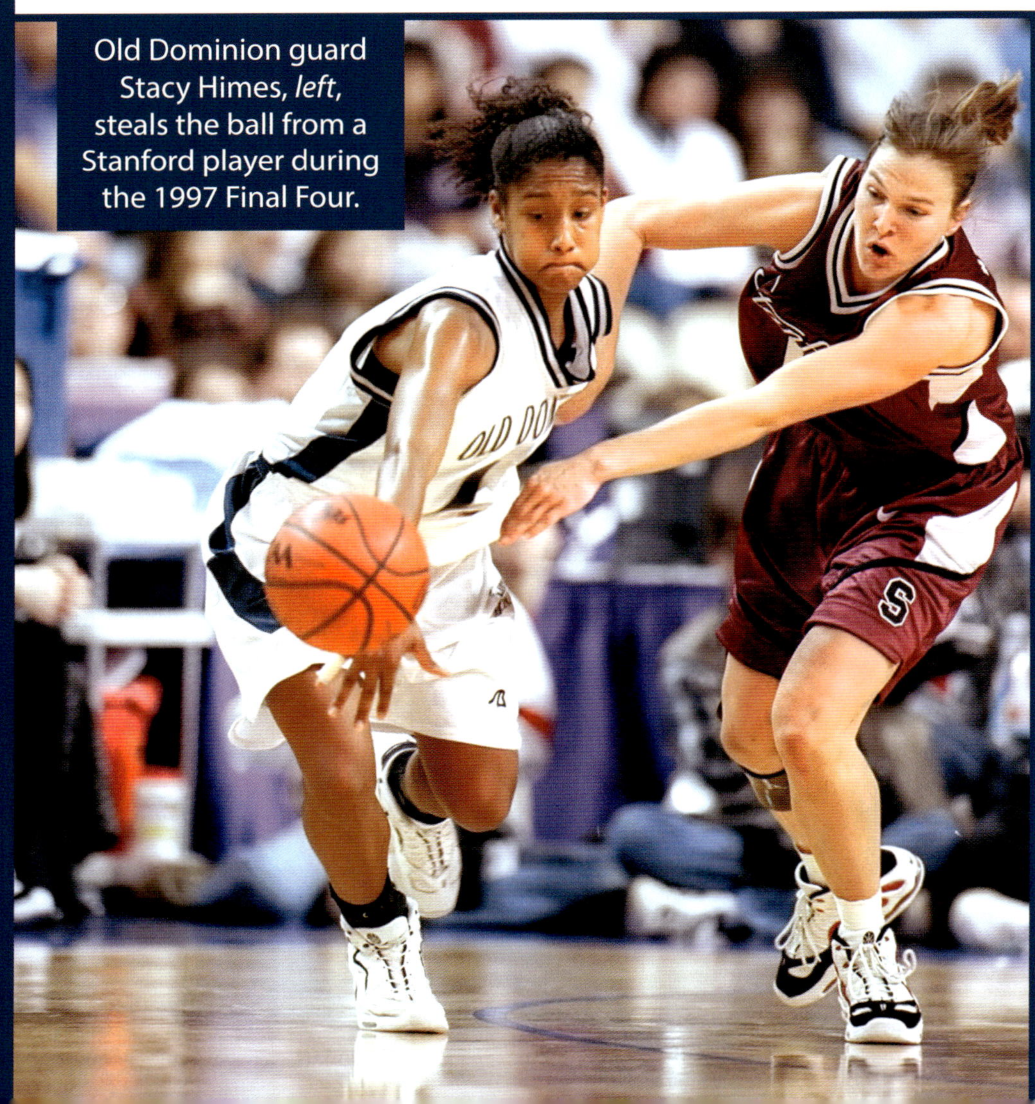


Old Dominion guard Stacy Himes, *left*, steals the ball from a Stanford player during the 1997 Final Four.

championship game. Facing Georgia, Dixon and Claxton combined to score 35 points and grab 35 rebounds. With a 70–65 win, Old Dominion claimed the team's first NCAA title.

Marianne Stanley had coached the Monarchs during their brightest seasons, from 1977 to 1987. New coach Wendy Larry kept the team competitive. From 1988 to 2008, the Monarchs missed only one NCAA Tournament. In 1997, they went on a 33-game winning streak. It included an 83–82 win over Stanford in the Final Four. However, Tennessee defeated Old Dominion 68–59 in the title game.

After 24 seasons, Larry stepped down in 2011. Old Dominion hoped to quickly snap a two-year streak of missing the NCAA Tournament. However, by 2025 that streak had reached 17 seasons.

## FACT BOX

**First Season:** 1969–70

**Location:** Norfolk, Virginia

**Arena:** Chartway Arena

**Conference:** Sun Belt Conference

**All-Time Record:** 1,183–518

**NCAA Tournament Appearances:** 25

**Final Fours:** 3

**National Titles:** 1979,* 1980,* 1985

**Top Coaches:** Marianne Stanley (1977–87); Wendy Larry (1987–2011)

**Top Players:** Nancy Lieberman (1976–80); Inge Nissen (1976–80); Anne Donovan (1979–83); Medina Dixon (1982–85); Tracy Claxton (1983–85); Ticha Penicheiro (1994–98); Clarisse Machanguana (1994–97); Nyree Roberts (1994–98)

**Mascot:** Big Blue

*AIAW

Oregon had played three seasons with part-time coaches before hiring Elwin Heiny to take on the full-time role in 1976. The investment soon paid off. By his third season, the Ducks emerged as the top team in the Northwest Basketball League. With six conference titles in eight years, Oregon became a regular in the AIAW and then NCAA tournaments.

Oregon point guard Sabrina Ionescu won the Naismith Award as the sport's best player in 2019–20.

By the late 1980s, however, the team began to fade. By the time Heiny left in 1993, his teams had missed the NCAA Tournament six years in a row. New coach Jody Runge quickly turned things around. In eight seasons, her teams made eight NCAA Tournaments. Still, the Ducks never got past the second round. Things got worse in Oregon before they got better. From 2002 to 2016, the Ducks made the NCAA Tournament only one time.

Oregon's turnaround began in 2014 when

the school hired coach Kelly Graves. Prior to his third season, Graves brought in a pair of top recruits in point guard Sabrina Ionescu and forward Ruthy Hebard. The freshman stars not only lifted Oregon back to the NCAA Tournament in 2017 but also guided the Ducks all the way to the Elite Eight. And they were only getting started.

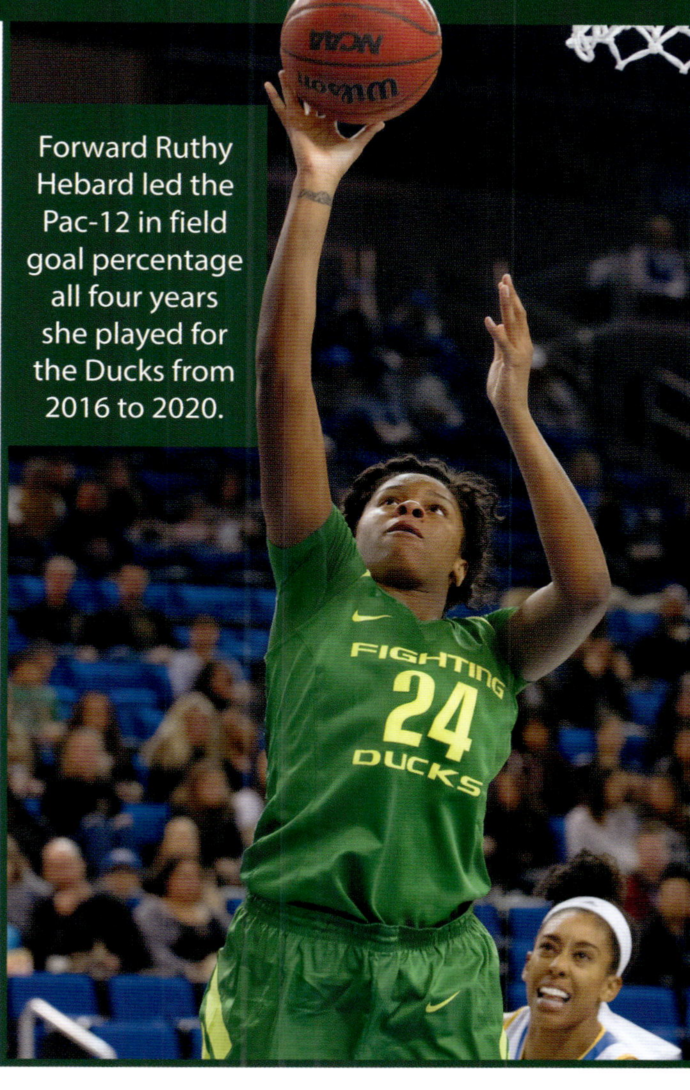


Forward Ruthy Hebard led the Pac-12 in field goal percentage all four years she played for the Ducks from 2016 to 2020.

The sharpshooting Ionescu quickly emerged as one of the nation's top players. Hebard complemented her with strong inside play. Together they led the Ducks back to the Elite Eight in 2018. By their junior season in 2018–19, another weapon emerged for Oregon in sophomore forward Satou Sabally. The three stars guided Oregon to its third straight Elite Eight. Then the trio combined to score 67 points against Mississippi State to send the Ducks to their first Final Four.

Expectations for 2019–20 were sky-high, and Oregon got off to a good start. Behind Ionescu, Hebard, and Sabally, the Ducks had the country's highest-scoring offense. For a time, they were also the top-ranked team in the country. However, they never got a chance to finish the job.

The Ducks recorded their 19th straight win when they beat Stanford in the Pac-12 Tournament championship game. At 31–2, they were ranked No. 2 in the country. But soon after, the COVID-19 pandemic spread across the country. As a result, the NCAA Tournament was canceled. Ionescu and Hebard moved on to the WNBA after that. While the Ducks remained competitive in the years that followed, they were no longer top contenders.

Oregon forward Satou Sabally earned All-America honors during her junior year in 2019–20.

## TRIPLE-DOUBLE MACHINE

On November 27, 2016, in just her seventh college game, Oregon's Sabrina Ionescu recorded 11 points, 12 rebounds, and 11 assists in a blowout win over San Jose State. That marked only the fifth triple-double in Oregon history and the first since 1988. During her junior year, Ionescu tallied her thirteenth triple-double. That set the record for the most triple-doubles in college basketball history, for women or men. Ionescu finished her career with 26 of them.

## FACT BOX

**First Season:** 1973–74

**Location:** Eugene, Oregon

**Arena:** Matthew Knight Arena

**Conference:** Big Ten Conference

**All-Time Record:** 912–602

**NCAA Tournament Appearances:** 18

**Final Fours:** 1

**National Titles:** None

**Top Coaches:** Elwin Heiny (1976–93); Kelly Graves (2014– )

**Top Players:** Bev Smith (1978–82); Stefanie Kasperski (1986–90); Shaquala Williams (1998–03); Jillian Alleyne (2012–16); Ruthy Hebard (2016–20); Sabrina Ionescu (2016–20); Satou Sabally (2017–20)

**Mascot:** The Oregon Duck

# OREGON STATE BEAVERS

In 2023–24, coach Scott Rueck, *left*, won at least 20 games in a season for the ninth time with Oregon State.

Aki Hill became Oregon State's coach ahead of the program's third season in 1978–79. Over the next six seasons, the Beavers reached the AIAW or NCAA tournament four times. The team's best run under Hill came in 1983, when it beat UCLA in the opening round. However, the Beavers soon fell off. Oregon State went nine seasons without reaching another NCAA Tournament.

The team enjoyed a brief resurgence at the end of Hill's tenure. From 1994 to 1996, Oregon State made two NCAA Tournaments under Hill and then another under new coach Judy Spoelstra. However, the Beavers then went 17 years without another berth.

In 2010–11, Scott Rueck took over as Oregon State's coach. With an emphasis on high-pressure defense, the Beavers soon began finding success again. By 2014, the Beavers were back in the NCAA Tournament. A year later, Oregon State won the Pac-12 regular-season title for the first time.

The Beavers defended their conference title in 2015–16 and entered the NCAA Tournament as a No. 2 seed. In the Sweet 16, Pac-12 Player of the Year Jamie Weisner racked up 38 points and ten rebounds to take down DePaul. The Beavers then beat Baylor 60–57 to advance to their first Final Four. Two years later, the Beavers went on another run. This time they beat Baylor 72–67 in the Sweet 16 to reach the Elite Eight.

Oregon State was ranked as high as No. 3 in the nation in 2019–20. However, there was no NCAA Tournament due to the COVID-19 pandemic. The Beavers then fell short of the tournament in 2022 and 2023.

Oregon State guard Jamie Weisner earned All-America honors as a senior in 2015–16.

All-American Raegan Beers sparked the team in 2023–24. The sophomore forward averaged a double-double during the season. In the Sweet 16, her 18 points and 13 rebounds sparked the No. 3 seed Beavers in an upset over No. 2 seed Notre Dame. Eventual champion South Carolina finally ended Oregon State's run with a 70–58 defeat in the Elite Eight.

Raegan Beers earned All–Pac-12 honors in her only two seasons at Oregon State, in 2022–23 and 2023–24.

## NO STOPPING HAMBLIN

Oregon State played in its first Pac-12 Tournament championship game in 2014. The Beavers lost to USC. Two years later, Ruth Hamblin wouldn't let them lose again. Facing UCLA, Hamblin scored 23 points and grabbed 20 rebounds. Her performance lifted the Beavers to their first conference tournament title.

## FACT BOX

**First Season:** 1976–77

**Location:** Corvallis, Oregon

**Arena:** Gill Coliseum

**Conference:** West Coast Conference

**All-Time Record:** 806–649

**NCAA Tournament Appearances:** 14

**Final Fours:** 1

**National Titles:** None

**Top Coaches:** Aki Hill (1978–95); Scott Rueck (2010– )

**Top Players:** Carol Menken (1978–81); Tanja Kostic (1992–96); Ruth Hamblin (2012–16); Jamie Weisner (2012–16); Sydney Wiese (2013–17); Raegan Beers (2022–24)

**Mascot:** Benny Beaver

# PURDUE BOILERMAKERS

Purdue created its women's basketball team in 1975. Early on, the Boilermakers struggled to contend in the Big Ten. That began to change when Lin Dunn took over as coach in 1987.

In her second season, Purdue reached its first NCAA Tournament. One year later, the Boilermakers got all the way to the Sweet 16. Having Joy Holmes helped. The forward went on to win Big Ten Player of the Year honors as a senior in 1990–91. Purdue won its first Big Ten regular-season title that year too.

Purdue guard Stephanie White won the Big Ten Player of the Year Award in 1998–99.

After missing the NCAA Tournament in 1993, Purdue came back with its best season yet in 1993–94. With four future WNBA players on the team, Purdue earned a No. 1 seed in the NCAA Tournament. Then the Boilermakers ripped off four wins to reach their first Final Four. Their closest win was by 17 points. However, the run ended with an 89–74 loss to North Carolina in the national semifinal. Purdue then got back to the Elite Eight in 1995. But after the team lost in the first round of the 1996 tournament, the school fired Dunn.

Carolyn Peck coached the team for just two seasons. The 1997–98 season ended with Purdue's first Big Ten Tournament title. The Boilermakers then made a run to the Elite Eight.

The next season was even better. The backcourt duo of Stephanie White and Katie Douglas led Purdue into the NCAA Tournament on a 26-game winning streak. The Boilermakers then won every tournament game by at least 13 points to reach the championship game. With four minutes left in the game against Duke, White went down with an injury. But behind senior guard Ukari Figgs, the Boilermakers rallied to beat the Blue Devils 62–45 and win their first national title.

Purdue guard Katie Douglas led the Big Ten in scoring in 1999–2000 with 20.4 points per game.

Peck left to coach in the WNBA, while White and Figgs graduated. Douglas stepped up into a bigger role. She won Big Ten Player of the Year honors in each of the next two seasons. In 2001, the Boilermakers got back to the NCAA title game. Down two against Notre Dame, Douglas heaved a shot just before

Starting in 2001–02, Purdue forward Shereka Wright earned All-America honors three years in a row.

the final buzzer sounded. The ball rattled off the rim to sink the Boilermakers' hopes of another title. Though Purdue reached the NCAA Tournament in 12 of the next 13 seasons, the team returned just once from 2018 to 2025.

## QUEENS OF THE BIG TEN

In 2013, Purdue won the Big Ten Tournament for the ninth time. At that point, no other team had won it more than three times. As of 2025, Purdue's nine titles were still the most in conference history.

## FACT BOX

**First Season:** 1975–76

**Location:** West Lafayette, Indiana

**Arena:** Mackey Arena

**Conference:** Big Ten Conference

**All-Time Record:** 948–575

**NCAA Tournament Appearances:** 27

**Final Fours:** 3

**National Titles:** 1999

**Top Coaches:** Lin Dunn (1987–96); Carolyn Peck (1997–99); Sharon Versyp (2006–21)

**Top Players:** Joy Holmes (1987–91); MaChelle Joseph (1988–92); Stacey Lovelace (1992–96); Stephanie White (1995–99); Ukari Figgs (1995–99); Katie Douglas (1997–2001); Shereka Wright (2000–04); Katie Gearlds (2003–07)

**Mascots:** Boilermaker Special and Purdue Pete

# RUTGERS SCARLET KNIGHTS

Coach Theresa Grentz guided Rutgers to each of the last four AIAW Tournaments, from 1979 to 1982. The Scarlet Knights got all the way to the championship game in 1982. The opposing Texas Longhorns entered the game on a 32-game winning streak. But thanks to a career-high 30 points from senior guard Patty Coyle, Rutgers won 83–77 to claim its first national title.

In 1982, Rutgers joined both the NCAA and the Atlantic 10 Conference. Three years later, the Scarlet Knights went undefeated in conference play and qualified for their first NCAA Tournament. From 1986 to 1994, Rutgers never missed the tournament. Star forward Sue Wicks led the team to the Elite Eight in 1986 and 1987.

After missing the 1995 tournament, Grentz left for a new job. The Scarlet Knights needed two seasons to settle in under new coach C. Vivian Stringer. Her arrival also marked Rutgers's first season in the Big East Conference. Before long, the team was a Big East power.

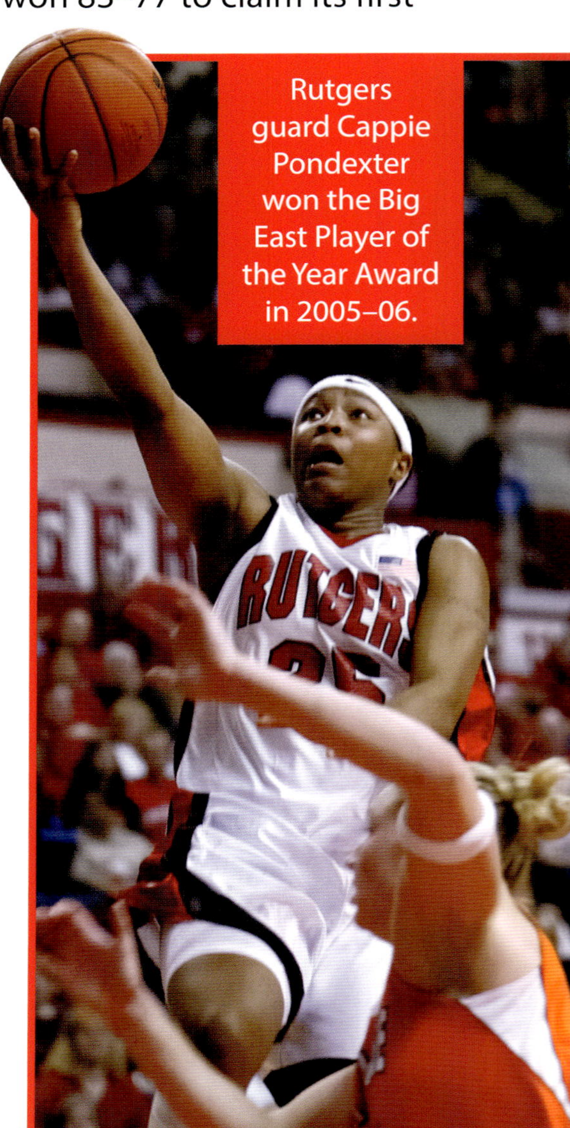

Rutgers guard Cappie Pondexter won the Big East Player of the Year Award in 2005–06.

Guard Epiphanny Prince earned All-America honors twice at Rutgers, in 2007–08 and 2008–09.

Under Stringer, the Scarlet Knights became a force defensively. That showed throughout the 2000 NCAA Tournament. In the Elite Eight, Rutgers shut down Georgia 59–51. That set up a date with Tennessee, winners of three straight NCAA titles from 1996 to 1998. Once again the Scarlet Knights played well defensively. However, the offense couldn't keep up in a 64–54 loss.

The Scarlet Knights' Big East rivals, the UConn Huskies, ended up winning the 2000 national title. Then they won three

### UNSTOPPABLE SEASON

As a senior in 1987–88, Sue Wicks led the Atlantic 10 with averages of 25.6 points, 12.1 rebounds, and 2.6 blocks. That helped her win the Naismith Award. Wicks finished her career as the leading scorer and rebounder in Rutgers history.

more from 2002 to 2004. Just when UConn was looking unbeatable, guard Cappie Pondexter helped lift Rutgers back to a pair of Big East regular-season titles in 2004–05 and 2005–06. Then the Scarlet Knights beat UConn to

C. Vivian Stringer celebrates after her 1,000th career win as a head coach. She retired in 2022 with 1,055 wins, including 547 while at Rutgers.

win their first Big East Tournament title in 2007. That began an amazing postseason run. Entering the NCAA Tournament as a No. 4 seed, Rutgers rode a stout defense all the way to the national title game. However, in the final, it was Tennessee that dominated defensively in a 59–46 Lady Vols win.

Rutgers enjoyed some of its best seasons under Stringer. However, around the time Rutgers joined the Big Ten in 2014, the team began to fall off. By the time Stringer retired in 2022, Rutgers had made the tournament only three times in the previous ten seasons.

## FACT BOX

**First Season:** 1974–75

**Location:** New Brunswick, New Jersey

**Arena:** Jersey Mike's Arena

**Conference:** Big Ten Conference

**All-Time Record:** 1,025–539

**NCAA Tournament Appearances:** 26

**Final Fours:** 2

**National Titles:** 1982*

**Top Coaches:** Theresa Grentz (1976–95); C. Vivian Stringer (1995–2022)

**Top Players:** Kris Kirchner (1980–81); June Olkowski (1978–82); Terry Dorner (1980–82); Sue Wicks (1984–88); Cappie Pondexter (2002–06); Epiphanny Prince (2006–09); Kahleah Copper (2012–16); Tyler Scaife (2013–18)

**Mascot:** Sir Henry, the Scarlet Knight

*AIAW

# SOUTH CAROLINA GAMECOCKS

In 2025, Dawn Staley, *second from left*, led South Carolina to its fifth straight Final Four.

South Carolina had appeared in six NCAA Tournaments prior to joining the SEC in 1991–92. After joining the SEC, the Gamecocks then went 11 years without returning to the Big Dance. The team enjoyed a brief resurgence in the early 2000s, including a run to the 2002 Elite Eight. But that led to another eight-year run of missing the tournament altogether.

In 2008, South Carolina hired Dawn Staley as coach. During her playing days, the two-time Naismith Award winner had been known for her defense. She brought that same attitude to her coaching. Before long, she was building a new power in South Carolina.

The team's NCAA Tournament drought ended in 2012. The Gamecocks weren't just happy to be there, though. They reached the Sweet 16. Two years later, South Carolina again

## PACKING THEM IN

As South Carolina became a winning team, it also became a popular team. The Gamecocks averaged 16,437 fans at home games in 2024–25. That set a program record. It also marked the 11th season in a row in which South Carolina led the nation in attendance.

got that deep in the tournament. Then, the 2015 team made a run all the way to the Final Four. Two-time SEC Player of the Year Tiffany Mitchell and star freshman A'ja Wilson led the way.

The 2017 tournament was South Carolina's fourth in a row as a No. 1 seed. Wilson, then a junior, was dominant. The 6-foot-5-inch forward and South Carolina native led the team to

South Carolina forward A'ja Wilson (22) celebrates winning the 2017 NCAA championship.

its first NCAA title game. Facing upstart Mississippi State, she recorded her third double-double of the tournament. South Carolina won easily, 67–55.

The Gamecocks had achieved a major turnaround under Staley. Wilson, the 2017–18 Naismith Award winner, played a big role. Then forward Aliyah Boston kept it going. The five-star recruit arrived in 2019–20. The Gamecocks were 32–1 in her freshman year when COVID-19 ended the season early. She never missed the Final Four after that. As a junior in 2021–22,

Starting in 2019–20, forward Aliyah Boston earned All-America honors all four years she played at South Carolina.

Boston won the Naismith Award while leading South Carolina to another national title.

After another trip to the Final Four in 2023, the Gamecocks reached the 2024 title game undefeated. Senior center Kamilla Cardoso made sure they finished the job. Her 15 points and 17 rebounds lifted South Carolina to an 87–75 win over Iowa. Staley guided her team back to the title game in 2025. It was the Gamecocks' third appearance in four years. However, this time they lost 82–59 to UConn.

## FACT BOX

**First Season:** 1974–75

**Location:** Columbia, South Carolina

**Arena:** Colonial Life Arena

**Conference:** Southeastern Conference

**All-Time Record:** 1,055–539

**NCAA Tournament Appearances:** 21

**Final Fours:** 7

**National Titles:** 2017, 2022, 2024

**Top Coaches:** Dawn Staley (2008– )

**Top Players:** Sheila Foster (1978–82); Shannon Johnson (1992–96); Tiffany Mitchell (2012–16); A'ja Wilson (2014–18); Tyasha Harris (2016–20); Aliyah Boston (2019–23); Zia Cooke (2019–23); Kamilla Cardoso (2020–24)

**Mascot:** Cocky

# STANFORD CARDINAL

Stanford made the first women's NCAA Tournament in 1982. At the time, postseason appearances were rare for the Cardinal. Soon after Tara VanDerveer took over as coach in 1985–86, NCAA Tournament berths became the norm.

In 1989–90, senior guard Jennifer Azzi won the Naismith Award. Stanford entered the NCAA Tournament as a No. 1 seed for the first time. The Cardinal then cruised through the tournament. They clinched their first national championship with an 88–81 win over Auburn in the title game.

Stanford continued its dominance in the early 1990s. After falling in the Final Four in 1991, the Cardinal returned to the championship game in 1992. Clamping down on defense, Stanford held Western Kentucky to under 30 percent shooting. That led to a 78–62 win for the Cardinal.

Tara VanDerveer, *center*, coached Stanford to 15 conference tournament titles from 1985 to 2024.

In 1996–97, senior forward Kate Starbird won the Naismith Award. She also led Stanford to the Final Four for the third year in a row. After losing in the national semifinals the previous two years, the Cardinal had a golden opportunity to beat Old Dominion. Instead, they missed three shots in the final 15 seconds and lost 83–82.

For the next decade, Stanford was unable to make a deep tournament run. Behind senior forward Candice Wiggins, that changed in 2008. The four-time All-American led Stanford to the Final Four. Then she put up 25 points and grabbed 13 rebounds in a win over UConn. However, Stanford fell to Tennessee in the championship game.

That season marked the start of five straight Final Four

Stanford guard Jennifer Azzi won Pac-10 Player of the Year honors in 1988–89 and 1989–90.

## OGWUMIKE SISTERS

Nneka Ogwumike arrived at Stanford in 2008–09. Her younger sister, Chiney, joined her two years later. Both skilled forwards, Nneka and Chiney each went on to become a three-time All-American. The Cardinal reached five Final Fours with an Ogwumike sister.

Forward Nneka Ogwumike, *right*, starred at Stanford from 2008 to 2012, while her sister and fellow forward Chiney Ogwumike was there from 2010 to 2014.

appearances for Stanford. The Cardinal advanced to the title game once, in 2010. That time they fell to UConn.

Stanford's next great run came in 2020–21. The Cardinal swept the Pac-12 regular-season and tournament titles for the first time in eight years. In the NCAA Tournament, sophomore guard Haley Jones scored 24 points against South Carolina in the Final Four. Then she put up 17 against Arizona to clinch Stanford's third national title.

VanDerveer retired after the 2023–24 season. In her 38 years, Stanford reached 14 Final Fours and won three national titles. When she retired, no college basketball coach had more than her 1,216 wins. Without her, the team's streak of 36 straight NCAA Tournament berths ended in 2025.

## FACT BOX

**First Season:** 1974–75

**Location:** Stanford, California

**Arena:** Maples Pavilion

**Conference:** Atlantic Coast Conference

**All-Time Record:** 1,256–373

**NCAA Tournament Appearances:** 37

**Final Fours:** 15

**National Titles:** 1990, 1992, 2021

**Top Coaches:** Tara VanDerveer (1985–2024)*

**Top Players:** Jennifer Azzi (1986–90); Kate Starbird (1993–97); Nicole Powell (2000–04); Candice Wiggins (2004–08); Nneka Ogwumike (2008–12); Chiney Ogwumike (2010–14); Haley Jones (2019–23); Cameron Brink (2020–24)

**Mascot:** The Tree (unofficial)

*VanDerveer missed the 1995–96 season to coach the US Olympic women's basketball team.

# SYRACUSE ORANGE

Muriel Smith coached the Syracuse Orange for their first seven seasons. In 1974–75, she led Syracuse to a perfect 10–0 record. However, the Orange didn't play in any postseason tournament that year.

In 1982–83, Syracuse joined the Big East. Two years later, the Orange won their only Big East Tournament title. In their first NCAA Tournament appearance, Syracuse lost to Old Dominion in the first round. Three years later, the Orange won their first Big East regular-season title. Back in the NCAA Tournament, Syracuse lost its first game again. The Orange didn't return to the tournament for 14 years.

Quentin Hillsman took over as Syracuse's coach for the 2006–07 season. The Orange still hadn't won a game in the NCAA Tournament. The drought finally

Syracuse guard Brittney Sykes earned All-ACC honors in 2013–14 and 2016–17.

ended in 2014.

Sophomore guards Brianna Butler and Brittney Sykes each recorded double-doubles to lift Syracuse to a 59–53 win against Chattanooga.

In 2015, Alexis Peterson led the Orange to another tournament win. The sophomore guard scored 24 points in a 72–69 win over Nebraska. She and the Orange were even better in the 2016 tournament. After winning in the first two rounds, Syracuse faced No. 1 seed South Carolina in the Sweet 16. Peterson poured in 26 points in an upset win. Then she scored 29 points in a blowout win against Tennessee. The win sent Syracuse to its first Final Four.

The ACC named Syracuse guard Alexis Peterson its Player of the Year in 2016–17.

## BUCKET GETTER

Before the 2022–23 season, Dyaisha Fair transferred to Syracuse. The senior guard had been one of the top scorers in the country at Buffalo. For two years, she led the Orange in scoring. In the first round of the 2024 NCAA Tournament, Fair scored 32 points to lead Syracuse to a win over Arizona. Fair finished her career with 3,403 points, the third-most in NCAA history.

Guard Dyaisha Fair averaged 21 points per game during her two years at Syracuse, starting in 2022–23.

The semifinal wasn't close. Peterson, Butler, and Sykes totaled 47 points in an 80–59 win over Washington. However, the magic stopped in the championship game against UConn. The Huskies beat Syracuse 82–51.

In 2021, the Orange reached their eighth NCAA Tournament in a row. However, Hillsman resigned after that amid allegations of inappropriate behavior. In 2024–25, the Orange posted their second losing record in four seasons.

## FACT BOX

**First Season:** 1971–72

**Location:** Syracuse, New York

**Arena:** JMA Wireless Dome

**Conference:** Atlantic Coast Conference

**All-Time Record:** 803–679

**NCAA Tournament Appearances:** 13

**Final Fours:** 1

**National Titles:** None

**Top Coaches:** Quentin Hillsman (2006–21)

**Top Players:** Kayla Alexander (2009–13); Brianna Butler (2012–16); Brittney Sykes (2012–17); Alexis Peterson (2013–17); Tiana Mangakahia (2017–21); Dyaisha Fair (2022–24)

**Mascot:** Otto the Orange

# TENNESSEE LADY VOLUNTEERS

Though Tennessee began a women's basketball program in 1903, the team didn't begin playing an official schedule until the 1974–75 season. The school hired a 22-year-old named Pat Summitt to guide the Lady Volunteers. A former star player at Tennessee-Martin, Summitt was ultracompetitive and demanded a lot from her players. Most importantly, she won.

Over her first 12 seasons, the Lady Vols reached seven Final Fours across the AIAW and NCAA tournaments. They finally won it all in 1987. Tennessee dominated Louisiana Tech 67–44 in the title game. Before long, the Lady Vols were the nation's premier team, with two more national titles in 1989 and 1991.

In 1995, UConn stopped Tennessee from winning a fourth title. That title-game showdown kicked off the sport's most famous rivalry. Behind the play of star freshman forward Chamique Holdsclaw, the Lady Vols got revenge against the

Legendary coach Pat Summitt, *center*, won 84 percent of her games at Tennessee from 1974 to 2012.

Huskies in the 1996 Final Four. Then they stomped Georgia to win another championship. Tennessee successfully defended that title in 1997.

By 1997–98, Holdsclaw was dominant. An all-around talent, she won the first of back-to-back Naismith Awards that season. She also got some help in the form of freshman forward Tamika Catchings. The pair led the Lady Vols to a perfect 39–0 season and a third straight championship.

With six national titles in 12 seasons, Tennessee was on top of the basketball world. Then defensive ace Catchings won the Naismith Award in 1999–2000. But the rivalry with UConn was turning. The Huskies beat Tennessee for that year's national title. They ended the Lady Vols' season in the Final Four or title

Tennessee forward Chamique Holdsclaw led the SEC in scoring as a sophomore in 1996–97. She then repeated the feat again the next two seasons.

## HISTORIC SLAM

Candace Parker took college basketball by storm as a freshman in 2005–06. In her first NCAA Tournament game, she capped off a fast break with a dunk. She became the first woman to dunk in an NCAA Tournament game. Later in the game, Parker dunked again.

game again in 2002, 2003, and 2004.

Candace Parker helped the Lady Vols return to the top. The dominant 6-foot-4-inch forward led Tennessee to back-to-back championships in 2007 and 2008. She earned the Naismith Award in the latter season.

Facing health problems, Summitt retired in 2012 at age 59. Over 38 seasons, her teams reached 22 Final Fours and won eight national titles.

Forward Candace Parker earned All-America honors all three years she played at Tennessee, starting in 2005–06.

Her 1,098 wins were the most in college basketball history at the time. Many consider Summitt one of the most important figures in the history of women's sports.

Rebuilding after Summitt was never going to be easy. The Volunteers have continued to be a winning team, though. In 2025, they continued their streak of appearing in the NCAA Tournament every year it's been held. That included three trips to the Sweet 16 in four years from 2022 to 2025.

## FACT BOX

**First Season:** 1903

**Location:** Knoxville, Tennessee

**Arena:** Thompson-Boling Arena

**Conference:** Southeastern Conference

**All-Time Record:** 1,495–395

**NCAA Tournament Appearances:** 43

**Final Fours:** 18

**National Titles:** 1987, 1989, 1991, 1996, 1997, 1998, 2007, 2008

**Top Coaches:** Pat Summitt (1974–2012)

**Top Players:** Bridgette Gordon (1985–89); Daedra Charles (1988–91); Nikki McCray (1991–95); Chamique Holdsclaw (1995–99); Tamika Catchings (1997–2001); Semeka Randall (1997–2001); Candace Parker (2005–08); Shekinna Stricklen (2008–12)

**Mascot:** Smokey

# TEXAS LONGHORNS

Texas went more than 20 seasons without experiencing a losing season. Jody Conradt played a big role in that. The school hired her as coach in 1976, before the team's third season. Conradt guided Texas to three straight AIAW Tournaments starting in 1980. High-scoring freshman center Annette Smith led the Longhorns all the way to the 1982 championship game, but Texas lost to Rutgers 83–77.

Texas coach Jody Conradt, *left*, was voted into the Basketball Hall of Fame in 1998.

Texas continued to win upon joining the NCAA the next season. Behind freshman forward Clarissa Davis, the Longhorns rolled through their opponents in 1985–86 and entered the NCAA Tournament undefeated. They remained unbeaten on their way to the championship game. There, they faced a strong USC team that had won national titles in 1983 and 1984. This one was all Texas, though. Davis scored a team-high 24 points in a 97–81 win. That made Texas the first women's team to finish an NCAA season undefeated.

Davis only got better from there. She won the Naismith Award in 1986–87 and 1988–89. However, she wasn't able to lift the Longhorns to another national title. Their best showing was another trip to the Final Four in 1987.

The Longhorns never made it past the Sweet 16 in the 1990s. All-America forward Stacy Stephens helped them finally break through to the Final Four

## REVENGE GAME

Texas entered the 1985 NCAA Tournament as a No. 1 seed. In the Sweet 16, Western Kentucky upset Texas 92–90. The two teams matched up again in the 1986 Final Four. This time, Texas had Clarissa Davis. The freshman star recorded 32 points and 18 rebounds in a 90–65 Texas win.

Texas teammates lift up forward Clarissa Davis after the Longhorns won the 1986 NCAA championship.

Forward Madison Booker won the SEC Player of the Year Award in 2024–25, the first year Texas played in the conference.

in 2003. Texas nearly reached the title game too. However, the team's buzzer-beater missed, and UConn won 71–69.

After 31 years at Texas, Conradt retired following the 2006–07 season. The Longhorns remained a consistent tournament team after she left. Texas began making deep runs again when Vic Schaefer took over before the 2020–21 season. In three of his first four years, the Longhorns made the Elite Eight. Then, in the 2025 NCAA Tournament, All-America sophomore forward Madison Booker led Texas to its first Final Four in 22 years.

## FACT BOX

**First Season:** 1974–75

**Location:** Austin, Texas

**Arena:** Moody Center

**Conference:** Southeastern Conference

**All-Time Record:** 1,251–445

**NCAA Tournament Appearances:** 37

**Final Fours:** 4

**National Titles:** 1986

**Top Coaches:** Jody Conradt (1976–2007); Vic Schaefer (2020– )

**Top Players:** Annette Smith (1981–86); Kamie Ethridge (1982–86); Clarissa Davis (1985–89); Edwina Brown (1996–2000); Stacy Stephens (2000–04); Tiffany Jackson (2003–07); Charli Collier (2018–21); Madison Booker (2023– )

**Mascot:** Hook 'Em

# TEXAS A&M AGGIES

Heading into the 1993–94 season, the Texas A&M Aggies had played 19 seasons and never appeared in a major postseason tournament. Even when they finally made the NCAA Tournament for the first time that spring, they did so as a No. 13 seed. But the Aggies got hot. Behind sophomore guard Lisa Branch, they upset No. 4 seed Florida and No. 5 seed San Diego State to reach the Sweet 16.

Branch continued to propel Texas A&M's offense for the next two seasons. In 1995, the Aggies won the WNIT. A year later, the Aggies won their first conference tournament title and

Coach Gary Blair won more than 70 percent of his games at Texas A&M from 2003 to 2022.

Aggies center Danielle Adams averaged 20.2 points per game during the 2011 NCAA Tournament.

returned to the Big Dance. However, without Branch, the team didn't return to the NCAA Tournament for another ten years.

The drought ended in 2006 under third-year coach Gary Blair. And just like that, a new streak began. Texas A&M went on to make 15 straight appearances in the tournament. The most successful of those seasons came with Danielle Adams

## FINAL FOUR THRILLER

In the 2011 Final Four, No. 1 seed Stanford led Texas A&M by 10 points with six minutes left. Then the Aggies started pressing on defense. By forcing turnovers, Texas A&M clawed its way back. With 3.3 seconds left, junior guard Tyra White made a layup to give the Aggies a 63–62 lead. They held on to clinch the upset.

Texas A&M center Kelsey Bone averaged 14.3 points and 8.1 rebounds at Texas A&M in 2011–12 and 2012–13.

roaming the court. The center arrived as a junior in 2009–10 and immediately led the Aggies to a second Big 12 Tournament championship in three years. Though they fell in the second round of the NCAA Tournament, the Aggies quickly bounced back in 2010–11. This time, the Aggies broke through to their first Final Four. Then they beat Stanford to reach the title game. Adams, then a senior, scored 30 points in a 76–70 win against Notre Dame to secure the Aggies' first championship.

## FACT BOX

**First Season:** 1974–75

**Location:** College Station, Texas

**Arena:** Reed Arena

**Conference:** Southeastern Conference

**All-Time Record:** 908–667

**NCAA Tournament Appearances:** 18

**Final Fours:** 1

**National Titles:** 2011

**Top Coaches:** Gary Blair (2003–22)

**Top Players:** Lisa Branch (1992–96); Takia Starks (2005–09); Danielle Adams (2009–11); Kelsey Bone (2011–13); Courtney Walker (2012–16); Chennedy Carter (2017–20)

**Mascot:** Reveille

In 2012–13, the Aggies joined the SEC. Behind All-America center Kelsey Bone, they won the SEC Tournament title. A year later, high-scoring guard Courtney Walker led the team to the Elite Eight.

Blair retired in 2022 after 19 seasons at Texas A&M. That February, the school named the court at Reed Arena after him. Blair won a school-record 444 games and led the Aggies to 16 NCAA Tournament appearances.

# TEXAS TECH LADY RAIDERS

In her second season coaching Texas Tech, Marsha Sharp led the Lady Raiders to the 1984 NCAA Tournament. It was their first trip to the Big Dance. They went back three more times over the next seven seasons. However, the team didn't win its first tournament game until forward Sheryl Swoopes arrived.

The Texas native transferred to Texas Tech before her junior season in 1991–92. As the nation's leading scorer with 21.6 points per game, Swoopes earned All-America honors. And she led the Lady Raiders not only to their first NCAA Tournament win but also eventually all the way to the Sweet 16.

The following year, Swoopes was even better.

Marsha Sharp coached Texas Tech to five conference tournament titles from 1982 to 2006.

She led the nation with 28.1 points per game and earned the Naismith Award. In the NCAA Tournament, she dropped at least 30 points in each game to lift the Lady Raiders to the championship game. Then she put up 47 points on Ohio State. That set an individual scoring record for the title game. It also proved to be just enough for Texas Tech to win 84–82 and claim its first national title.

Swoopes finished her career as one of the most dominant college players ever. Replacing her was never going to be easy. Center Michi Atkins had been a freshman on the 1993 title-winning team. She went on to become an All-American, and the Lady Raiders got to a pair of Sweet 16s plus an Elite Eight in her three remaining seasons.

Alicia Thompson and Angie Braziel carried Texas Tech after that. The Big 12 named Thompson, a 6-foot-1-inch forward, its Player of the Year

Forward Sheryl Swoopes averaged 24.9 points per game at Texas Tech in 1991–92 and 1992–93.

## RECORD SCORERS

Three Texas Tech players have scored at least 2,000 points. Center Michi Atkins finished her career in 1996 with 2,134 points. Two years later, forward Alicia Thompson dropped 39 points in an NCAA Tournament game to pass Atkins. Thompson finished her career with 2,156 points. However, neither could catch center Carolyn Thompson. She scored 2,655 from 1980 to 1984.

Texas Tech players celebrate after defeating New Mexico in the 2003 NCAA Tournament.

in 1997–98. The conference gave that honor to Braziel, a 6-foot-3-inch center, the following year. The Lady Raiders swept the Big 12 regular-season and tournament titles both seasons.

All the while, Texas Tech kept reaching the NCAA Tournament. The Lady Raiders got back to the Elite Eight in 2000 and 2003. The 2005 tournament was their sixteenth in a row under Sharp. That streak came to an end the next year. Sharp also retired following that 2005–06 season, her 21st leading the team. Under Sharp, the Lady Raiders had reached ten Sweet 16s. Maintaining that success proved difficult. Texas Tech reached just two NCAA Tournaments in the first 19 seasons after Sharp left. Both ended in first-round exits.

## FACT BOX

**First Season:** 1975–76

**Location:** Lubbock, Texas

**Arena:** United Supermarkets Arena

**Conference:** Big 12 Conference

**All-Time Record:** 1,002–601

**NCAA Tournament Appearances:** 20

**Final Fours:** 1

**National Titles:** 1993

**Top Coaches:** Marsha Sharp (1982–2006)

**Top Players:** Carolyn Thompson (1980–84); Krista Kirkland (1989–93); Sheryl Swoopes (1991–93); Michi Atkins (1992–96); Alicia Thompson (1994–98); Plenette Pierson (1999–2003)

**Mascot:** Raider Red

# UCLA BRUINS

The UCLA Bruins have played at Pauley Pavilion since their first season in 1974–75.

When the University of California, Los Angeles (UCLA) Bruins played their first season in 1974–75, they had a freshman star ready to light up Pauley Pavilion. Shooting guard Ann Meyers had been the first high schooler to play for the US national team. Upon joining the Bruins, Meyers went on to earn All-America honors in all four of her seasons.

Meyers was hardly the Bruins' only star, though. She regularly set up fellow guard Anita Ortega to score. In 1977–78,

UCLA guard Jordin Canada led the Pac-12 in steals and assists in the 2016–17 season.

freshman forward Denise Curry racked up rebounds. That same season was coach Billie Moore's first at UCLA. With a loaded roster, Moore led UCLA to the AIAW Final Four at Pauley Pavilion.

After beating Montclair State 85–77 in the semifinal, the Bruins dominated Maryland in the final. Meyers, by then a senior, recorded 20 points, ten rebounds, nine assists, and eight steals. With a 90–74 win, UCLA claimed its first national title.

Even without Meyers in 1978–79, the Bruins remained strong. Ortega and Curry led the team back to the Final Four. But Old Dominion beat the Bruins 87–82.

The success didn't continue into the NCAA era, though. From 1982 to 2015, UCLA made the NCAA Tournament only 12 times. It got as far as the Elite Eight only once, in 1999.

The Bruins finally began putting together a new era of success when coach Cori Close arrived in 2011–12. After reaching one NCAA Tournament in her first four seasons, the Bruins missed just one between 2016 and 2024. In 2018, All-America guard Jordin Canada lifted

UCLA center Lauren Betts was named the Naismith Defensive Player of the Year in 2024–25.

## HISTORIC PLAYER

Ann Meyers had a groundbreaking career at UCLA. She became the first female athlete to receive a full athletic scholarship at any school. On the court, she set 12 team records. In one 1978 game, she recorded a quadruple-double. That had never been done before in college basketball. She also won a silver medal with Team USA at the 1976 Olympics. Meyers was later enshrined in the Basketball Hall of Fame.

UCLA all the way to the Elite Eight.

Behind juniors Lauren Betts and Kiki Rice, UCLA took another step in 2024–25. After starting the season 23–0, the Bruins won the Big Ten Tournament title in the school's first year in the conference. For the first time, UCLA earned a No. 1 seed in the NCAA Tournament. Then, in the Elite Eight, Betts blocked six shots against LSU to send the Bruins to their first Final Four in the NCAA era.

## FACT BOX

**First Season:** 1974–75

**Location:** Los Angeles, California

**Arena:** Pauley Pavilion

**Conference:** Big Ten Conference

**All-Time Record:** 978–569

**NCAA Tournament Appearances:** 19

**Final Fours:** 1

**National Titles:** 1978*

**Top Coaches:** Billie Moore (1977–93); Cori Close (2011– )

**Top Players:** Ann Meyers (1974–78); Anita Ortega (1975–79); Denise Curry (1977–81); Natalie Williams (1990–94); Maylana Martin (1996–2000); Jordin Canada (2014–18); Michaela Onyenwere (2017–21); Lauren Betts (2023– )

**Mascot:** Joe and Josephine Bruin

*AIAW

# USC TROJANS

Linda Sharp became coach of the University of Southern California (USC) Trojans in 1977–78, the program's second season. Following a run to the AIAW Final Four in 1981, Sharp led the Trojans to the Elite Eight in the first NCAA Tournament in 1982. Soon, a hotshot recruit lifted USC to even greater heights.

USC forward Cheryl Miller earned All-America honors all four years at USC.

California native Cheryl Miller once scored 105 points in a high school game. The 6-foot-3-inch forward quickly began piling up points in college too. As a USC freshman in 1982–83, Miller averaged 20.4 points per game to earn All-America honors.

## CHAMPION TWINS

Cheryl Miller carried the Trojans throughout her career. However, in the 1984 championship game, twin sisters Pamela and Paula McGee starred for USC. Each scored a team-high 17 points, helping the Trojans defend their national title.

USC met Louisiana Tech for the national title. The Lady Techsters had won 30 games in a row. Behind a game-high 27 points from Miller, USC ended that streak and claimed its first championship.

As a sophomore, Miller won her first of three straight Naismith Awards. And she led the Trojans back to the championship game. This time, the Trojans defeated rising power Tennessee to win the title.

The Trojans lost in the Sweet 16 in 1985, but Miller took them back to the 1986 Final Four. There, the Trojans easily beat Tennessee in the semifinals. However, Miller's historic college career ended with a loss to Texas in the title game.

Center Lisa Leslie led the Pac-10 in blocks in all four seasons she played at USC, starting in 1990–91.

Another California native starred at USC in the early 1990s. Center Lisa Leslie dominated in the paint on offense and defense, earning the Naismith Award in 1993–94. She shared the frontcourt with freshman Tina Thompson, a rising star.

USC guard JuJu Watkins scored 920 points in 2023–24, the most ever by a freshman.

And with Miller back on the bench as coach, USC reached the Elite Eight.

Miller led the Trojans back to the NCAA Tournament in 1995 before leaving to work as a broadcaster. Success proved hard to come by after that. USC made only four NCAA Tournaments between 1996 and 2022. Once again, a local star came in to lift the program.

Los Angeles native JuJu Watkins was the country's top recruit. She lived up to the hype in 2023–24, earning All-America honors as a freshman. The dynamic guard then led USC to its first Elite Eight in 30 years.

## FACT BOX

**First Season:** 1976–77

**Location:** Los Angeles, California

**Arena:** Galen Center

**Conference:** Big Ten Conference

**All-Time Record:** 903–561

**NCAA Tournament Appearances:** 19

**Final Fours:** 3

**National Titles:** 1983, 1984

**Top Coaches:** Linda Sharp (1977–89)

**Top Players:** Pamela McGee (1981–84); Paula McGee (1981–84); Cynthia Cooper (1981–86); Cheryl Miller (1982–86); Cherie Nelson (1985–89); Lisa Leslie (1990–94); Tina Thompson (1993–97); JuJu Watkins (2023– )

**Mascot:** Tommy Trojan

Watkins was even better the next year and won the Naismith Award. Many thought she could lead the No. 1 seed Trojans to a national title. However, those hopes took a hit when Watkins was injured in the second round of the tournament. Without their star, the Trojans lost in the Elite Eight.

# UTAH UTES

Fern Gardner took over as Utah's coach before the team's second season in 1975–76. In her first two years, the Utes went 45–8 and reached back-to-back AIAW Tournaments. In 1982–83, high-scoring junior forward Deb Asper helped the Utes reach their first NCAA Tournament.

Gardner left after that. The winning seasons continued under new coach Elaine Elliott. She led the Utes to six NCAA

Coach Elaine Elliott won 582 games while at Utah from 1983 to 2010.

Tournaments in her first 14 seasons. However, Utah still hadn't gotten out of the first round. That finally changed in 1997. The Utes beat Iowa State 66–57 to pick up their first win in the Big Dance.

Before the 1999–2000 season, Utah joined the Mountain West Conference. In 2000–01, the Utes finished the season 14–0 in conference play. Behind an elite defense, Utah reached the Sweet 16 for the first time.

Forward Kim Smith averaged 17.5 points per game during her career at Utah from 2002–03 to 2005–06.

Kim Smith helped Utah go on another tournament run in 2006. The four-time Mountain West Player of the Year tallied 25 points and nine rebounds in the second round to lead Utah into the Sweet 16. There, the Utes beat Boston College 57–54 to advance to their first Elite Eight. Smith recorded a double-double with 17 points and 18 rebounds against Maryland. But Utah lost in overtime.

Utah forward Alissa Pili won Pac-12 Player of the Year honors in 2022–23.

## BIG-GAME PLAYER

Before the 2022–23 season, forward Alissa Pili transferred from USC to Utah. The Alaska native thrived on her new team, averaging more than 20 points per game during both of her seasons with Utah. She played even better in the Big Dance. In five NCAA Tournament games with the Utes, Pili averaged 27.2 points.

Elliott stepped down after the 2009–10 season. She left as the winningest coach in Mountain West history. Two years later, Utah joined the bigger Pac-12 Conference.

The program struggled in the wake of those changes. Utah went 11 years without making the NCAA Tournament. That streak finally ended in 2022. The Utes had less trouble adjusting to another conference in 2024–25. In its first year in the Big 12, Utah made its fourth straight NCAA Tournament.

## FACT BOX

**First Season:** 1974–75

**Location:** Salt Lake City, Utah

**Arena:** Jon M. Huntsman Center

**Conference:** Big 12 Conference

**All-Time Record:** 1,030–509

**NCAA Tournament Appearances:** 21

**Final Fours:** None

**National Titles:** None

**Top Coaches:** Fern Gardner (1975–83); Elaine Elliott (1983–2010)

**Top Players:** Deb Asper (1980–84); Anne Handy (1981–85); Julie Krommenhoek (1994–98); Kim Smith (2002–06); Shona Thorburn (2002–06); Leilani Mitchell (2007–08); Michelle Plouffe (2010–14); Alissa Pili (2022–24)

**Mascot:** Swoop

# VIRGINIA CAVALIERS

Debbie Ryan coached Virginia to 11 regular-season ACC titles from 1977 to 2011.

Virginia cycled through two coaches in its first four seasons. Before the fifth in 1977–78, the Cavaliers hired Debbie Ryan. Virginia didn't need a new coach again for more than 30 years.

In 1983–84, Ryan helped Virginia win the ACC regular-season title for the first time. The Cavaliers followed that up with their first trip to the NCAA Tournament. Two years later, Virginia topped the ACC standings again and earned a No. 1 seed for the 1986 NCAA Tournament. However, No. 8 seed James Madison upset the Cavaliers in the second round.

Dawn Staley helped end Virginia's NCAA Tournament woes. As a sophomore, the tenacious guard lifted the Cavaliers to

## DOMINANT IN DEFEAT

In the 1991 national championship game, Dawn Staley recorded 28 points, 11 rebounds, six assists, and three steals. Her stellar performance still wasn't enough to beat Tennessee. Nonetheless, Staley became the first player to be named Final Four Most Outstanding Player without winning the tournament.

their first Final Four in 1990. To get there, they beat defending champion Tennessee in overtime in the Elite Eight. A year later, Virginia took down UConn in the Final Four. In their first national title game, the Cavaliers again faced Tennessee. Once again the teams needed overtime to decide a winner. But this time, the Lady Vols won 70–67.

Staley won her second straight Naismith Award

Virginia guard Dawn Staley led the ACC in assists and steals during her junior and senior seasons in 1990–91 and 1991–92.

in 1991–92. All that was missing was a national championship. In the Final Four, Virginia trailed Stanford 66–65 with less than a second left. Staley received an inbounds pass but couldn't get a shot off in time.

## FACT BOX

**First Season:** 1973–74

**Location:** Charlottesville, Virginia

**Arena:** John Paul Jones Arena

**Conference:** Atlantic Coast Conference

**All-Time Record:** 993–564

**NCAA Tournament Appearances:** 25

**Final Fours:** 3

**National Titles:** None

**Top Coaches:** Debbie Ryan (1977–2011)

**Top Players:** Donna Holt (1984–88); Tammi Reiss (1988–92); Dawn Staley (1988–92); Heather Burge (1989–93); Wendy Palmer (1992–96); Sharnee Zoll (2004–08); Lyndra Littles (2005–09); Monica Wright (2006–10)

**Mascot:** Cavman

The Cavaliers continued to dominate in the ACC. Forward-center Wendy Palmer arrived in 1992–93. She went on to become a two-time ACC Player of the Year. As a senior in 1995–96, Palmer led Virginia to its sixth consecutive ACC regular-season title. The Cavaliers also reached three Elite Eights in her career. However, they couldn't break through to another Final Four.

Following her 34th season, Ryan retired in 2011. She finished her career at Virginia with 739 wins and 24 NCAA Tournament appearances. After Ryan retired, Virginia made the Big Dance just once in the next 14 seasons.

Forward-center Wendy Palmer's 1,124 rebounds from 1992 to 1996 were the most in Virginia's history.

# VIRGINIA TECH HOKIES

Under coach Carol Alfano, Virginia Tech experienced many firsts. During her second season as coach, in 1979–80, Alfano led the Hokies to their first winning season. Alfano guided them to their first NCAA Tournament in 1994. One year after that, the Hokies won the Metropolitan Collegiate Athletic Conference regular-season title for the first time. They carried that momentum into the NCAA Tournament and beat Saint Joseph's 62–52 for their first NCAA Tournament win.

Bonnie Henrickson took over for Alfano before the 1997–98 season. During her seven years in charge, the Hokies made five NCAA Tournament appearances. That included a run to the Sweet 16 in 1999. However, postseason success dried up after Henrickson left in 2004. Starting in 2007, the Hokies went 14 years without making the NCAA Tournament.

Kenny Brooks began rebuilding the program. He took over as coach in

Virginia Tech's HokieBird mascot traces its history back to 1962.

## LONG TIME COMING

By 2022–23, Virginia Tech had played in the ACC for 19 years. Yet the Hokies had never advanced to the ACC Tournament championship game. That finally changed in 2023. Virginia Tech beat Louisville 75–67 to win its first ACC Tournament title. Georgia Amoore and Elizabeth Kitley scored a combined total of 45 points in the title game.

2016 and immediately led the Hokies to four straight winning seasons. The next step was returning to the NCAA Tournament.

Center Elizabeth Kitley and guard Georgia Amoore were instrumental in changing that. In 2021, they led the Hokies back to the NCAA Tournament. And once there, Virginia Tech even won a game.

Virginia Tech guard Georgia Amoore's 6.8 assists per game led the ACC in 2023–24.

Hokies center Elizabeth Kitley earned All-America honors in 2021–22 and 2022–23.

The Hokies kept improving. In 2023, they entered the NCAA Tournament as a No. 1 seed for the first time, and then they made a run to their first Elite Eight. Facing Ohio State, Kitley recorded a double-double of 25 points and 12 rebounds. Amoore added 24 points. Their performances lifted Virginia Tech to an 84–74 win and a berth in the Final Four.

Virginia Tech's run ended with a 79–72 loss to eventual champion LSU. But with Kitley and Amoore back, the Hokies looked to build on that success in 2024. Virginia Tech won its first ACC regular-season title, while Kitley earned her third straight ACC Player of the Year Award. However, a knee injury ended her season, and without her the Hokies lost in the second round of the NCAA Tournament. Kitley, Amoore, and Brooks all left after that, and Virginia Tech's run of four straight NCAA Tournament berths ended in 2025.

## FACT BOX

**First Season:** 1976–77

**Location:** Blacksburg, Virginia

**Arena:** Cassell Coliseum

**Conference:** Atlantic Coast Conference

**All-Time Record:** 821–641

**NCAA Tournament Appearances:** 13

**Final Fours:** 1

**National Titles:** None

**Top Coaches:** Carol Alfano (1978–97); Kenny Brooks (2016–24)

**Top Players:** Lisa Witherspoon (1995–99); Tere Williams (1997–2001); Regan Magarity (2014–19); Aisha Sheppard (2017–22); Elizabeth Kitley (2019–24); Georgia Amoore (2020–24)

**Mascot:** HokieBird

# WASHINGTON HUSKIES

Harry the Husky has been Washington's mascot since 1995.

The Washington Huskies experienced many changes in their early years as a program. After playing their first three seasons as an independent, the Huskies joined the National Women's Basketball League before the 1977–78 season. Five years later, Washington became part of the North Pacific Conference (NorPac).

By the mid-1980s, the Huskies were regular NCAA Tournament qualifiers. They missed only one tournament between 1985 and 1996. Most of that success came under coach Chris Gobrecht.

Gobrecht took over in 1985–86. That was also Washington's last year in the NorPac before joining the Pac-10. Over Gobrecht's first ten seasons, the Huskies reached the NCAA Tournament nine times. Their best run came in 1990. As a No. 1 seed, the Huskies reached the

Guard Jazmine Davis made an All–Pac-12 team during each of her four years at Washington, from 2011–12 to 2014–15.

Elite Eight before falling to No. 2 seed Auburn. After missing the tournament for only the second time in 1996, Gobrecht left to coach Florida State.

For the next 11 seasons, Washington had mixed success under coach June Daugherty. Her best season came in 2000–01. That year, the No. 6 seed Huskies reached the Elite Eight. However, they lost to Southwest Missouri State.

Washington fired Daugherty after a first-round loss in the 2007 NCAA Tournament. Instead of getting better, the Huskies got worse. After six seasons without another tournament berth, the school hired Mike Neighbors. He brought a game-changing recruit with him.

Kelsey Plum, a 5-foot-8-inch guard from Southern California, shined from the start. She set Washington's single-season scoring record as a freshman in 2013–14. By her sophomore year, the Huskies were back in the NCAA Tournament.

Things really took off for Washington in the 2016 NCAA Tournament. As a No. 7 seed, the Huskies held off Penn, then upset No. 2 seed Maryland, No. 3 Kentucky, and No. 4 Stanford. Facing No. 4 Syracuse in the Final Four, Huskies senior forward Talia Walton hit eight three-pointers to set a Final Four record. However, Syracuse otherwise dominated the Huskies in an 80–59 win.

Plum finished that season as the nation's third-leading scorer. As a senior, she led the country with 31.7 points per game. However, all her baskets couldn't get the Huskies past the Sweet 16. Both she and Neighbors left after that 2016–17 season. The Huskies didn't get back to the NCAA Tournament until 2025, their first year in the Big Ten Conference.

Guard Kelsey Plum averaged 25.4 points per game over her career at Washington from 2013 to 2017.

## SUPER SENIOR

Washington guard Kelsey Plum proved to be a dominant scorer throughout her time in Seattle. On February 25, 2017, she had a chance to make history. With Utah in town for Plum's final regular-season game, the senior star needed 54 points to surpass 3,393 and become the NCAA's all-time leading scorer. She scored a career-best 57 in an 84–77 win. Plum went on to finish her career with 3,527 points. She also set the NCAA single-season scoring record as a senior with 1,109 points. It was little surprise when she ended her college career by winning the Naismith Award.

## FACT BOX

**First Season:** 1974–75

**Location:** Seattle, Washington

**Arena:** Hec Edmundson Pavilion

**Conference:** Big Ten Conference

**All-Time Record:** 917–605

**NCAA Tournament Appearances:** 20

**Final Fours:** 1

**National Titles:** None

**Top Coaches:** Chris Gobrecht (1986–96); Mike Neighbors (2013–17)

**Top Players:** Rhonda Banchero (1991–95); Jamie Redd (1995–99); Giuliana Mendiola (2000–04); Jazmine Davis (2011–15); Talia Walton (2011–16); Chantel Osahor (2013–17); Kelsey Plum (2013–17)

**Mascot:** Harry the Husky

# ALL-TIME NCAA RECORDS

## CAREER RECORDS

**Points**
Caitlin Clark, Iowa (2020–24): 3,951

**Rebounds**
Courtney Paris,
Oklahoma (2005–09): 2,034

**Assists**
Suzie McConnell,
Penn State (1984–88): 1,307

**Steals**
Chastadie Barrs, Lamar (2015–19): 649

**Blocks**
Brittney Griner, Baylor (2009–13): 748

**Three-Pointers Made**
Caitlin Clark, Iowa (2000–24): 548

**Free Throws Made**
Kelsey Plum,
Washington (2013–17): 912

## SINGLE-SEASON RECORDS

**Points**
Caitlin Clark, Iowa (2023–24): 1,234

**Rebounds**
Natalie Butler,
George Mason (2017–18): 563

**Assists**
Courtney Vandersloot,
Gonzaga (2010–11): 367

**Steals**
Chastadie Barrs, Lamar (2018–19): 193

**Blocks**
Brittney Griner, Baylor (2009–10): 223

**Three-Pointers Made**
Taylor Pierce, Idaho (2018–19): 154

**Free Throws Made**
Shala Dobbins, Prairie View (2017–18): 296

## SINGLE-GAME RECORDS

**Points**
Ayoka Lee, Kansas State (January 23, 2022): 61

**Rebounds**
Deborah Temple, Delta State (February 14, 1983): 40

**Assists**
Michelle Burden, Kent State (February 6, 1991): 23

**Steals**
Seven players with 14

**Blocks**
Sandora Irvin, TCU (January 16, 2005): 16
Brittany Brewer, Texas Tech (December 22, 2019): 16

**Three-Pointers Made**
Juicy Landrum, Baylor (December 18, 2019): 14

**Free Throws Made**
Kelsey Minato, Army (February 12, 2014): 26

## COACHING RECORDS

**Wins**
Geno Auriemma, UConn (1985– ): 1,250

**Finals Fours**
Geno Auriemma, UConn (1985– ): 24

**Championships**
Geno Auriemma, UConn (1985– ): 12

# GLOSSARY

### All-American
A player chosen as one of the best amateurs in the country in a particular sport.

### alum
A person who graduated from a particular school.

### berth
A spot in a competition or tournament earned through previous results.

### campus
The grounds of a school.

### clutch
Performing well in an important situation that often decides a competition or game.

### conference
A group of schools that join together to create a league for their sports teams.

### double-double
Accumulating ten or more of two certain statistics in a game.

### dynasty
A team that has an extended period of success, usually winning multiple championships in the process.

### inequities
Circumstances that are unfair or unjust.

### overtime
An extra period of play when the score is tied after regulation.

### pandemic
A widespread outbreak of a disease that affects a large portion of the population.

### recruit
A high school athlete that college teams try to persuade to join them.

### retire
To end one's career.

### rival
An opponent with whom a player or team has a fierce and ongoing competition.

### transfer
To move to a new school.

### triple-double
Accumulating ten or more of three certain statistics in a game.

### upset
An unexpected victory by a supposedly weaker team or player.

# TO LEARN MORE

## FURTHER READINGS

Beattie, Charlie. *The Men's College Basketball Encyclopedia*. Abdo, 2026.

Borzilleri, Meri-Jo. *Who Is Caitlin Clark?* Penguin Workshop, 2025.

Hanlon, Luke. *Everything Basketball*. Abdo, 2024.

## ONLINE RESOURCES

To learn more about women's college basketball, please visit **abdobooklinks.com** or scan this QR code. These links are routinely monitored and updated to provide the most current information available.

# INDEX

# PHOTO CREDITS

Cover Photos: Cover Photos: Shutterstock Images, front (hoop); Jessica Hill/AP Images, front (Maya Moore); Scott Taetsch/NCAA Photos/Getty Images, front (Angel Reese); G. Fiume/Getty Images Sport/Getty Images, front (Caitlin Clark); Keith Birmingham/MediaNews Group/Pasadena Star-News/Getty Images, front (JuJu Watkins); Alvin Chung/AP Images, front (Cheryl Miller); AP Images, back (Smith team)
Interior Photos: Brian Rothmuller/Icon Sportswire/Getty Images, 1, 166; Nell Redmond/AP Images, 2–3, 132, 134–135; Blanchard Harper/Wisconsin Historical Society/Archive Photos/Getty Images, 4; AP Images, 5; George Rinhart/Corbis Historical/Getty Images, 6; Bettmann/Getty Images, 8, 112; Old Dominion University Special Collections, 9; John Iacono/Sports Illustrated/Getty Images, 10; Jim Mone/AP Images, 11; Alvin Chung/AP Images, 12; Wade Payne/AP Images, 14; Mike Ehrmann/Getty Images Sport/Getty Images, 15; Sean Rayford/Getty Images Sport/Getty Images, 16; Matthew Holst/Getty Images Sport/Getty Images, 17; Joe Buglewicz/Getty Images Sport/Getty Images, 18–19; Jim Bryant/AP Images, 20; Carmen Mandato/Getty Images Sport/Getty Images, 21, 22; James A. Finley/AP Images, 24; Bob Jordan/AP Images, 25; Mark Humphrey/AP Images, 26, 145; Peter G. Aiken/Getty Images Sport/Getty Images, 28; Justin Edmonds/Getty Images Sport/Getty Images, 29, 185; Chris O'Meara/AP Images, 30; Elise Amendola/AP Images, 32, 187; Jessica Hill/AP Images, 33, 34; Robert W. Stowell Jr./Archive Photos/Getty Images, 36; Maddie Meyer/Getty Images, 36–37; Elsa/Getty Images Sport/Getty Images, 38, 62, 97, 153; Grant Halverson/Getty Images Sport/Getty Images, 39; Andy Mead/YCJ/Corbis/Icon Sportswire/Getty Images, 40–41, 141; Matthew Stockman/Getty Images Sport/Getty Images, 42; Jonathan Daniel/Getty Images Sport/Getty Images, 43; Jed Jacobsohn/Allsport/Getty Images Sport/Getty Images, 44; Michael Allio/Icon Sportswire/Getty Images, 46; Jaime Green/Wichita Eagle/Tribune News Service/Getty Images, 47; Charlie Neibergall/AP Images, 48, 50, 51; Steph Chambers/Getty Images Sport/Getty Images, 52–53, 98–99; Mitchell Layton/Getty Images Sport/Getty Images, 54; Austin Bachand/Daily News-Record/AP Images, 55; Pat Sullivan/AP Images, 56; Richard Mackson/Sports Illustrated/Getty Images, 58; Todd Warshaw/Allsport/Getty Images Sport/Getty Images, 59, 124, 175; Allison Long/Kansas City Star/Tribune News Service/Getty Images, 60; Doug Benc/Getty Images Sport/Getty Images, 63; Kevin C. Cox/Getty Images Sport/Getty Images, 64; Darron Cummings/AP Images, 66–67; Tom Pennington/Getty Images Sport/Getty Images, 67, 184; Doug Pizac/AP Images, 68; Peter Read Miller/Sports Illustrated/Getty Images, 69; Bill Haber/AP Images, 70; Kirby Lee/Getty Images Sport/Getty Images, 72, 152; Andy Lyons/Getty Images Sport/Getty Images, 73, 74–75, 86, 102, 108, 120; T. Quinn/WireImage/Getty Images Sport/Getty Images, 76; Jim McIsaac/Getty Images Sport/Getty Images, 77; G. Fiume/Maryland Terrapins/Getty Images Sport/Getty Images, 78, 140, 154; Al Goldis/AP Images, 80–81, 81, 82; Kiichiro Sato/AP Images, 84; Eric Gay/AP Images, 85; Andy Lyons/Allsport/Getty Images Sport/Getty Images, 88, 125; Jamie Schwaberow/NCAA Photos/Getty Images, 89; Matthew Putney/AP Images, 90; Andy Mead/YCJ/Icon Sportswire/Getty Images, 92; Marcy Nighswander/AP Images, 93; Max Turner/Icon Sport Media/Icon Sportswire/Getty Images, 94–95; Craig Jones/Allsport/Getty Images Sport/Getty Images, 96; Elsa/Allsport/Getty Images Sport/Getty Images, 100; Michael Hickey/Getty Images Sport/Getty Images, 101; Jay LaPrete/AP Images, 104; Jeff Zelevansky/Getty Images Sport/Getty Images, 105; Jeffrey Brown/Icon Sportswire/Getty Images, 106; J. Meric/Getty Images Sport/Getty Images, 109, 110–111; CRO/AP Images, 113; Jonathan Daniel/Getty Images Sport/Getty Images, 114; Ethan Miller/Getty Images Sport/Getty Images, 116, 118–119; David Dennis/Icon Sportswire/Getty Images, 117; Timothy J. Gonzalez/AP Images, 121; Tyler Schank/Clarkson Creative/Getty Images Sport/Getty Images, 122–123; Sandra Dukes/Getty Images Sport/Getty Images, 126; Tim Larsen/AP Images, 128; Richard Schultz/WireImage/Getty Images, 129; Mitchell Leff/Getty Images Sport/Getty Images, 130; Richard W. Rodriguez/Fort Worth Star-Telegram/Tribune News Service/Getty Images, 133; Cody Glenn/Icon Sportswire/Getty Images, 136; Otto Greule Jr./Getty Images Sport/Getty Images, 137; Doug Pensinger/Getty Images Sport/Getty Images, 138, 168; Lance King/Getty Images Sport/Getty Images, 142; Damian Strohmeyer/Allsport/Hulton Archive/Getty Images, 144, 173; Kelly Kline/Getty Images Sport/Getty Images, 146; Focus On Sport/Getty Images, 148; Gary Landers/AP Images, 149; Jay Biggerstaff/Getty Images Sport/Getty Images, 150; Amy Conn-Gutierrez/AP Images, 156–157; Amy Sancetta/AP Images, 157; Jake Schoellkopf/AP Images, 158; Katharine Lotze/Getty Images Sport/Getty Images, 160–161; David Dennis/Corbis/Icon Sportswire/Getty Images, 161; Patrick McDermott/Getty Images Sport/Getty Images, 162; Mike Powell/Getty Images Sport/Getty Images, 164; Ken Levine/Allsport/Getty Images Sport/Getty Images, 165; John Miller/AP Images, 169; M. Anthony Nesmith/Icon Sportswire/Getty Images, 170; Landon Nordeman/The Daily Progress/AP Images, 172; Al Bello/Getty Images Sport/Getty Images, 176; G. Fiume/Getty Images Sports/Getty Images, 177; Ryan Hunt/Getty Images Sport/Getty Images, 178; Jesse Beals/Icon Sportswire/Getty Images, 180, 182; Elaine Thompson/AP Images, 181

**ABDOBOOKS.COM**

Published by Abdo Reference, a division of ABDO, PO Box 398166, Minneapolis, Minnesota 55439. 

Printed in China.
102025
012026

Editor: Chrös McDougall
Series Designer: Colleen McLaren
Production Designer: Kate Liestman

**LIBRARY OF CONGRESS CONTROL NUMBER: 2025939306**

**PUBLISHER'S CATALOGING-IN-PUBLICATION DATA**

Names: Hanlon, Luke, author.
Title: The women's college basketball encyclopedia / by Luke Hanlon
Description: Minneapolis, Minnesota: Abdo Reference, 2026 | Series: College sports encyclopedias | Includes online resources and index.
Identifiers: ISBN 9781098298869 (lib. bdg.) | ISBN 9798384932666 (ebook)
Subjects: LCSH: Basketball--Juvenile literature. | Basketball for women--Juvenile literature. | College sports--Juvenile literature. | Basketball teams--Juvenile literature. | Sports--United States--History--Juvenile literature. | Encyclopedias--Juvenile literature.
Classification: DDC 796.323--dc23